OUT OF CONTROL

How the girls next door became the
world's most notorious sex criminals

OUT OF CONTROL

How the girls next door became the
world's most notorious sex criminals

Linda G. Stunell

ROBINSON
London

Constable & Robinson Ltd
3 The Lanchesters
162 Fulham Palace Road
London W6 9ER
www.constablerobinson.com

First published in the UK by Robinson,
an imprint of Constable & Robinson Ltd 2007

A copy of the British Library Cataloguing in
Publication data is available from the British Library

ISBN-13: 978-1-84529-509-7
ISBN-10: 1-84529-509-9

Printed and bound in the EU

1 3 5 7 9 10 8 6 4 2

CONTENTS

ILLUSTRATIONS

Female anatomy

John Bobbitt points during testimony in the sixth day of
Lorena Bobbitt's sexual abuse trial against him
© AP Photo/Scott Applewhite

The knife used by Lorena Bobbitt to cut off the penis of her
husband, John Bobbitt
© AP Photo/Steve Helber

John Bobbitt's severed penis
© Peter Heimsath/Rex Features

Lorena Bobbitt, flanked by her lawyers
© AP Photo/Scott Applewhite

Vili Fualaau with his lawyer Bob Huff
© Sipa Press/Rex Features

Mary Kay Letourneau in court
© Sipa Press/Rex Features

Pamela and Gregg Smart on their wedding day
© Sipa Press/Rex Features

Pamela Smart
© **Sipa Press/Rex Features**

William Flynn
© **Sipa Press/Rex Features**

Karla Homolka, Lori Homolka and father Karel Homolka
© **TS/Keystone USA/Rex Features**

Paul Bernardo in a police car
© **TS/Keystone USA/Rex Features**

A salesman watches an interview with Karla Homolka on television
© **AP/EMPICS photo by CP PHOTO/Ryan Remiorz**

Karla Faye Tucker
© **Sipa Press/Rex Features**

Melchora Vasquez, chief clerk for Harris County's trial exhibits, returns the pickaxe used by Karla Faye Tucker in the 1983 killing of Jerry Lynn Dean
© **AP/EMPICS photo by David J. Phillip**

George W. Bush
© **Ron Sachs/Rex Features**

1

THE GENDER WAR:
WHO'S WINNING?

'Every man I meet wants to protect me.
Can't figure out from what.'   *Mae West*

The reason why the serpent was included on the guest list when
God created the world remains an unsolved mystery. For the
movie and publishing industry, the serpent's presence in the
Garden of Eden was a mixed blessing. Without free will to
choose the path of unrighteousness, there would be no stories to
tell because there would be no villains to drive the plot.
Imagine *Fatal Attraction* without Alex, *Star Wars* without Darth
Vader, Dr Jekyll without Mr Hyde. If Eve hadn't eaten the
forbidden fruit and given birth to villainhood, the creators of
film and literature would have invented it. The Executive
Producer of life on Earth must have known that Eve and her evil
offspring were essential performers on the world stage and that
without them, the cast list would be incomplete.

Eve is the world's first and most powerful villain. She alone
is held responsible for humanity's downfall. Without her,
there would be no evil, no wars, no conflict and no vice. She
is carnal, tempting and sinful. By contrast, the Virgin Mary is
kind, pure and chaste. These gender splitting archetypes are
a root cause of gender war conflicts. Murder, rape and assault
are consequences.

MONSTERS AND VILLAINS

Bloodthirsty killers in maniac movies have been stalking the silver screen for close to a century. The personalities of most of Hollywood's movie villains and heroes are developmentally stunted at the level of two-year-olds. Like two-year-olds they love to destroy things, and people are no exception. Slasher movies pit powerful chest-beating heroes against powerful cut-throat villains in a blood fest of glorified violence. Villains thrill American audiences with the same, if not more enthusiasm than heroic cowboys, cops, soldiers and terminators. Jason in *Friday The 13th* is a typical monster villain. He is ruthless, glassy-eyed, sadistic, horny-for-blood and risen from the dead. Like the hero, he must be a worthy opponent: fearless, relentless, strong and determined.

Powerful male hero defeats powerful male monster, saves powerless female victim. This hero-monster-victim plot formula has served as the heartbeat of American movies since the birth of the industry. Male monsters, vampires, creatures, beasts, bastards, werewolves and psychopaths overpower, decapitate, dismember, rape, humiliate and bludgeon women to death. Female witches, bitches, vixens and whores tempt, trick, betray, harass, poison, seduce and sexually manipulate men to death.

HEROES AND HEROINES

The female heroine archetype is the princess-victim. She serves as a prop for men. Rose, (Kate Winslet) in the 200-million-dollar budget 1997 blockbuster, *Titanic*, exemplifies the female princess-victim archetype. She is young, pretty, powerless, desperate, helpless, suicidal and needs to be rescued by heart throb hero, Leonardo DiCaprio. Scarlett O'Hara is another princess-victim archetype. She is pretty, powerless, challengingly rebellious and in need of a rescuer. The morning after she is raped by a drunk and violent Rhett Butler, she awakens with an orgasmic smile on her face. The messages that the princess-victim archetype delivers to both male and female audiences is that women are helpless victims who need to be saved, rescued (and sometimes raped) by strong, invincible men and that a woman's power and success is only in relation to her consumer driven external beauty. Women who dare to behave like male heroes by being direct, fearless, assertive and confrontational are called 'ball breakers' and 'bitches' and demoted to the status of villain.

The male hero and the male villain are split archetypes that complete the hero-monster-victim psychic complex. *Batman* and *Superman*, *Hercules* and *Tarzan*, *Zorro* and *007* are invincible male action heroes who are so one dimensionally alike that when stripped of their capes, masks and loincloths, become clones of each other like Dolly the sheep. They are macho and fearless, tough and death-defying, powerful and virile. They don't need anybody, don't ask for help, never complain and survive physical challenges against impossible odds using superhuman strength. They rescue females in distress but are far too independent to form meaningful relationships.

By identifying with fairytale princesses in *Beauty and the Beast*, *Cinderella*, *Anastasia* and *Pocahontas*, girls grow up with the expectation that someday their one dimensional hero will come along, make their lives magically meaningful and rescue them from their empty, unfulfilled existences. Sooner or later, the perfect husband, provider, father, lover, protector and rescuer turns out to be three-dimensionally imperfect and they become disillusioned and resentful.

When the husbands of Pamela Smart and Lorena Bobbitt didn't measure up, one was murdered and the other suffered a fate worse than death.

Men who identify with male super hero role models by being tough, virile and in control, cut themselves off from their feelings. Like Rocky Balboa, they are supposed to beat the eight count and keep on punching. Women who try to live up to the cultural ideals of womanhood by being passively helpless and in need of a rescuer, cut themselves off from their power. Hero-rescuers and princess-victims polarize the genders and split their individual wholeness into separate parts. According to gender researchers Aaron Kipnis, PhD., and Elizabeth Herron, M.A., 'Problems arise when any one of these psychological elements dominates our character. We become possessed by the split-off part, which, in acting out its polarized role, is also constantly seeking its missing counter-part'. Women have a strong, capable and powerful heroic side. Men have a gentle, vulnerable, caring side. Becoming complete, multidimensional human beings means accepting our human flaws and imperfections and embracing the maleness and femaleness that exists in all of us. Denying these very real parts of ourselves is not only gender alienating and separating but self-alienating and separating.

Kipnis and Heron propose that the path to gender peace is reconnecting with the split-off parts of ourselves. Instead of identifying with a continuous stream of cartoonish, one-dimensional, consumer driven role models of manhood and womanhood, we need to reclaim ourselves as multidimensional human beings and confront the real monsters that need confronting — starving populations, ozone depletion and the extinction of species.

FROM PRINCESS-VICTIM TO OUTLAW-HERO

In 1991, the Hollywood movie industry experienced a cardiac arrest. Somebody reversed the gender formula. That somebody was renegade screenwriter, Callie Khourri, who wrote the Big Screen gender-bender, *Thelma and Louise* about a couple of outlaw women avenging sexist crimes with both barrels. 'Male-hero defeats male-villain and rescues female-victim' suddenly became 'female-heroes defeat male-villains and rescue themselves'.

When the film first opened, a posse of wounded male egos took aim and fired back. John Robinson of the Boston Globe called the movie 'the last straw . . . in a string of cultural strikes against manhood'. Bill Cosford of the *Miami Herald* condemned it as a 'butt kicking feminist manifesto'. In the *Nation*, Stuart Klawans wrote, 'Anger – that's the simmering element beneath this film – women's anger'. Joining the male protesters, columnist Ellen Goodman labelled it, 'A PMS movie, plain and simple'. In his book *The Myth Of Male Power*, Warren Farrell issued a warning that 'male bashing is everywhere . . . it would be a mistake to view the current situation as simply another skirmish in the war between the sexes . . . not with only one side showing up. Women have been doing the shooting and men have been burying their heads in the sand hoping the bullets will miss.' In an article for *MacLeans* magazine, Fred Bruning urged men to run for cover. 'Even if Farrell is correct, men probably do not deserve a break', Fred conceded. 'They have ruled the world and made an absolute mess of things. They have exploited. They have belched. They have consorted with floozies. Keep firing those shots, ladies. Boys, keep yourselves covered. This could last awhile.'

Not since blaxploitation and *The Spook Who Sat By The Door* had a movie injected itself into the national bloodstream and caused such energetic sabre rattling and table pounding. Director Ridley Scott defended the movie as 'not about rape. It's about choices and freedom.' Actor Susan Sarandon ('Louise'), who fired the controversial shot, called the movie a 'breakthrough . . . not only because two women are playing cowboys in "a cowboy movie with cars" but because it has an ending that is not the usual studio ending . . . My character had to be on a journey asking what makes women victims and why men feel they have a right to do this.'

In a damage control interview with the *New York Times*, screen writer Callie Khourri, declared that her movie wasn't hostile towards men. 'It's hostile towards idiots.' Khourri grew up seeing women portrayed in movies as sex objects, passive partners or terminally ill. 'As a female-movie goer, I just got fed up with the passive role of women. They were never driving the story because they were never driving the car.' Khourri saw complaints about the movie as a 'double standard'. She wanted a movie about women who make their own decisions and control their own destiny which meant inventing female characters who overstep the traditional behaviour boundaries assigned to women. She invented two free spirited, misbehaving outlaw-buddies, Thelma and Louise, who avenge sexist crimes in the American south-west with a posse of cop-mobiles on their trail. 'Thelma and Louise' became a powerful laxative for women's stuffed rage and symbolized a monumental turning point in gender politics.

UNSTUFFED

Thelma, played by Geena Davis, is a young, repressed, sub-servient housewife frozen in childlike dependency. She got married at age 18 to a redneck, philandering, cheating, buffoonish, dominating, ego-drunk, patronizing, tyrannical, narcissistic carpet salesman named Darryl who represents everything dumb and dumbest about traditional masculinity. 'He's an asshole,' says Thelma, 'but most times I just let it slide.' Her best buddy, Louise, works as a waitress in an Arkansas greasy spoon. She's ballsy, world-weary, wised up and fed up with her travelling musician boyfriend, Jimmy, who won't commit. Both women are due for a break from their boxed-in small town lives.

Louise arranges a weekend getaway at a friend's mountain cabin in her 1966 Thunderbird convertible. Thelma, who is afraid to ask Darryl for permission to go, leaves him a note and dinner in the microwave. With the radio blasting, the two women throw caution to the wind and burn a trail of rubber down the open highway. As they pass a western style honky-tonk road house called the Silver Bullet, Thelma coaxes Louise to make a pit stop. Inside the smoky haze of the Silver Bullet, Harlan Puckett, a cowboy-hustler-super-pig in his sexist prime, joins them uninvited. Harlan is a bar-room regular with pro-grammed expectations about his god given right to women's bodies. After knocking back three Wild Turkeys, Thelma joins Harlan for some foot-stomping country line dancing. Using booze and flattery, Harlan leads the tipsy Thelma outside into the parking lot for a sobering breath of fresh air. When she resists his advances, he bats her around like a rag doll and slams her face down over the hood of a parked car.

Louise arrives on the scene just as Harlan is about to rape Thelma – doggie-style. Louise retrieves Darryl's gun (the gun Thelma brought along for protection) and presses the barrel into Harlan's neck. 'Just for the future, when a woman's crying like that, she's not having any fun,' exclaims Louise with a tumbleweed accent. Harlan backs off and shouts, 'Suck my cock!' Louise, who had been previously traumatized by a similar event in Texas, blows the scumball away. 'You watch your mouth, buddy,' says Louise to the dead man. Dazed and shaken, the two women climb into the convertible and peel away. Louise, chain-smoking at the wheel of the car, decides to make a run for the Mexican border. The cops won't buy the truth, she tells Thelma. 'We just don't live in that kind of world . . . besides I don't want to end up on the damn Geraldo show.'

With the pedal to the floor, the women outlaws accelerate into a south-western widescreen landscape of big skies, red deserts and moonlit canyons where there's nothing between them and eternity except the horizon. From Arkansas to Arizona, they are on the run in a male world of shiny chrome tanker trucks, tractor trailers, spraying crop dusters and freight trains. They stop and pick up a sweet-talking hustler-hitchhiker (Brad Pitt) who introduces Thelma to orgasmic sex for the first time in her entire self-sacrificing, people-pleasing life. The guy is a convenience store bandit who teaches Thelma the art of grand larceny using her blow-dryer as an imaginary gun to demonstrate his skills. Louise contacts her musician boyfriend who delivers her life savings to her ($6,700) at a roadside motel. Thelma's bandit lover boy splits with the cash and leaves Thelma and Louise high and dry.

Thelma embarks on a new career – holding up convenience stores. She tells Louise, 'I know it's crazy. I just feel like I got a knack for this shit.' As the female desperados progress from crime to crime, they quickly shed their illusions about their need for male protectors. When a macho state trooper pulls them over along a deserted stretch of highway, the women disarm him, shoot out his police radio, stuff him in the trunk of his police car and throw away the keys. 'You be sweet to your wife,' warns Thelma, 'My husband wasn't sweet to me, and look how I turned out.'

When Thelma phones home, she finds out that police wire tappers have moved in with her husband, Darryl. A paternalistic detective comes on the line and tries to talk the women into giving themselves up. Fat chance. With pistols tucked in their dusty jeans, the lawless duo high tail it through the desert in their topless Thunderbird knocking back miniature bottles of Wild Turkey. A passing chauvinist halfwit driving a phallic chrome tanker truck wants to play fender tag and asks them if they're 'ready to get serious' as he vibrates and wiggles his protruding tongue at them and makes lewd gestures. Sick and tired of being treated like public property, the women pull over and give the trucker a lecture about harassing women and a chance to apologize. In the absence of an apology, they pump a round of bullets into the fuel truck, blow the rig sky high and leave their harasser in the dust screaming, 'Bitches from hell!'

The movie climaxes at the dead end rim of the grand canyon where an army of cop cars, guns and a helicopter close in on them. The women outlaws contemplate their last free choice. 'Let's not get caught,' urges Thelma. 'Go!' Like Butch Cassidy and the Sundance Kid who went out in a blaze of 'testosteronic' glory, Thelma and Louise step on the gas and lift off in a blaze of 'estrogenic' glory, proving they are strong. They are invincible. They are women.

In a scathing article for *People* magazine, Ralph Novak wrote, 'Any movie that went as far out of its way to trash women as this female chauvinist sow of a film does to trash men would be universally and justifiably condemned.' Kathio Maio of *Ms* magazine counter-punched with, 'Dream on, Ralph. Negative stereotyping of women is, indeed, the accepted norm in Hollywood films. And violence against women in slasher films and so-called thrillers constitutes a continuous stream of female blood. So, when this level of anti-feminist bombast is directed at one warm, often funny, ultimately tragic road picture, you can only conclude that though the guys like to dish it out, they sure can't take it . . . for once in a Hollywood film, men are held accountable for their oppression of women. And not just for the crime of rape . . . Thelma and Louise portrayed male violence as an ordinary, everyday event. It's more than rape. It's a husband's verbal abuse of his wife – it's a stranger feeling he has the right to harass any woman . . . '

What made Thelma and Louise such controversial movie heroines is that instead of modelling lingerie, they were modelling power in a language that men could understand. The movie struck a nerve for millions of women trapped in the quiet desperation of poor jobs, failing marriages and meat markets like the Silver Bullet. They could identify not just with the retaliatory anger that the characters expressed but with their deepest fears. For Thelma, that fear was growing old with a husband who didn't love her. For Louise, it was growing old alone.

SEXUAL ASSAULT IS LEARNED

Thelma and Louise kicked off a decade of gender war movies expressing a vindictive off-balance rivalry between the sexes. *The First Wives Club* with its hell-hath-no-fury theme teamed together three affluent, middle-aged divorcees who get mad and get even. A woman expresses judicious revenge towards a brutally perverse man in *Silence Of The Lambs*. In *Fatal Attraction*, a rejected mistress stalks, torments and turns a married man's life into a living hell.

Serial sex killer Karla Homolka was a devoted fan of the movie *Criminal Law* about a serial rapist (Kevin Bacon) who rapes young women, stuffs disposable diapers in their mouths, strangles and kills them, then lights their genitals on fire to destroy the forensic evidence. *Friday The 13th* was another of Karla's favourites. Both movies, which she rented repeatedly, taught her the ABCs of murder and violent sex. Her serial rapist boyfriend, Paul Bernardo, taught her the XYZs.

Pamela Smart's inspiration for child rape was Van Halen's heavy metal music. Nicknamed the 'Maiden of Metal', Pamela Smart seduced her 15-year-old student, Billy Flynn, to Van Halen's 'Hot For Teacher' which describes the seduction of a pupil by his teacher. Lorena Bobbitt and Karla Faye Tucker learned military combat techniques from their soldier partners. After years of verbal, physical and sexual abuse, both women turned their learned aggression (in the form of a kitchen carving knife and a pickaxe) on male victims. Mary Letourneau's role model father secretly sired two children with a young student mistress from a college where he taught philosophy.

Sexual assault is learned. It is learned from role models who teach by example. It is learned from the media who make celebrity superstars out of rapists and killers and sensationalize their crimes. It is learned from a cultural value system that polarizes, divides and alienates the genders through sex stereotyping. It is learned through pornography that depicts women as passive, submissive sex objects who desire abuse, even until death in some cases. While many women still feel that any challenge to male dominance is unfeminine, others are buying guns and strap-ons.

11

HOMOPHOBIA

'The compelling force behind sex role rigidity is homophobia,' says Del Martin in her book, *Battered Wives*. Gender stereotyping has been injected into public consciousness like a vaccine against homosexuality. The mistaken belief that sex roles determine sexuality and can cause a child to be homosexual is widespread.

Heterosexual roles emphasize the differences and divisions between men and women as 'opposite' sexes. The perception of women as the weaker sex contributes to men's contempt for everything feminine. Driven by fears of homosexuality, men repress human traits that might be labelled 'feminine' and become obsessed with their masculinity. Proving they're not sissys or queers is learned at the playground where aggressiveness is equated with male identity, power and the masculine ideal. Insecure men feel compelled to constantly prove their manhood by lashing out whenever they feel their masculinity is being challenged or threatened. 'An insecure man who hides his emotional fragility behind a tough exterior is complemented by the dependent female gender role. The two reinforce the dependent pathology of the other,' says sociologist, Freda Briggs.

'Sex in our age has become gladiatorial with male and female, gay and straight whipping and goading each other for position,' says Camille Paglia, author of *Vamps and Tramps*. Although men are conditioned to be virile and powerful, few get a chance to be Rambo. One male batterer with a failed Macho Complex explains that, 'Women don't realize the image us men get caught up in. We are supposed to be tough, don't show your feelings, and always be in charge. You gotta bring home the bread and please everybody . . . you get frustrated sometimes that you can't do it all.' Male rapists and batterers become violent in an effort to live up to a distorted ideal of manhood. Their abuse of women is a means of overcompensating for their inadequacy and a shortcut to being what they think they should be as men. The majority of male rapists and batterers perceive themselves as powerless and as failures in the male role.

HUMANIZATION

Sociologist Edgar Morin sees the feminization of men and the masculinization of women as a step on the way to human-ization. It provides an opportunity for both sexes to experience the complete cycle of humanity. 'There is no doubt', says Morin, 'that men "become humanized" when they develop their genetic and cultural femininity.' According to Morin, our sense of sexual identity is learned after birth and is culturally deter-mined. While certain behaviours are encouraged, others are discouraged. Everything including a child's name, clothes, games and toys play a role in a child's training and conditioning and serve to manipulate, modify and defy nature. Fuelled by a conditioned fear and intolerance of homosexuality, boys and girls are pressured to conform to these unnatural, culturally determined gender role stereotypes.

In her controversial book, *The Unopposite Sex*, Elisabeth Badinter asserts that the sexes are raised differently to prepare for separate destinies but 'in actual fact, we are all androgynous, because human beings are bisexual, on several levels and to different degrees'. Masculine and feminine are intertwined in all of us. Testosterone is not a male hormone. Estrogen is not a female hormone. Every living thing possesses masculine and feminine qualities. Badinter suggests that both homosexuality and heterosexuality cut us off from deep and important feelings for people of the same or opposite sex. The path to gender liberation, says Badinter, is to experience God, nature and soul as genderless.

According to bisexual poster boy Gore Vidal, 'Everybody is bisexual. Not that everyone practices it.' As entertainment celebrities George Michael, Elton John and Ellen DeGeneres came out of the closet and made 'gay okay', basketball pro, Denis Rodman, went into the closet – women's closets. Men of the twenty-first century are bleaching and manicuring, tanning and waxing, piercing and primping. They are donning earrings, jewellery, designer clothes and exotic fragrances. Women are wearing buzz-cuts, shirts, suits and ties and running corporations. Bi-curious men and women are satisfying their curiosity and discovering that bisexuality is not located somewhere between homosexuality and heterosexuality. It is a natural state of being that liberates them from artificial 'manly' and 'womanly' stereotypes and allows both genders to express the greatest possible resemblance as well as all possible differences.

FROM VICTIM PRINCESS TO WARRIOR PRINCESS

She set a precedent as 'the first mass murdering, bisexual, homeless woman to capture the hearts of American families'. Her name was Xena: Warrior Princess and she made *Thelma and Louise* look like a couple of nuns out on a Sunday drive. Played by 29-year-old New Zealander Lucy Lawless, Xena was a mythological gladiatrix and TV Titan with a celestial goddess-like beauty, a flashing broadsword, leather minidress, steel breastplate and 'chakram' – a razor sharp metal circlet that she hurled like a frisbee and that returned to her like a boomerang. She was the first take-no-crap, tall, kick-ass strong woman on TV. She was camp. She was vamp. She was sexy and testy. She was 'wonder woman' on steroids. She was a Joan of Arc/Aileen

14

Wuornos hybrid doing mid-air somersaults, decapitating people and vanquishing whoever got in her way. 'The fastest growing audience who are now taking control of the remote are women,' says Lawless. Six million viewers a week watched the grinning, sword wielding queen of prime time whose show became the most watched syndicated drama series on television. The show's openly gay producer, Liz Friedman, held nothing back. The rule for the series, said Friedman, was to write it no differently than if it were written for a man. Xena was not a character who role-modelled 'mass-cultural expectations of women'. She was a dark and dangerous sword and sorcerer princess who rode wild unicorns, ran with the gods and battled with gladiators. Her leaps and flips, flying fists and vicious leg kicks were accompanied by a high pitched animalistic wail that fans tried to ape . . . 'yi-yi-yi-yi-yi!'. Xena was the embodiment of centuries of historic injustice and pent-up feminist rage. She was a fighter and an adventurer and she was totally independent of men, yet straight men adored her. 'What's not to like?' says George, an online fan who watches Xena reruns. 'I watch her in action and I think . . . wow, could she kick my ass . . . and I kind of dig that.' Producer, Liz Friedman, admitted the teasing sexual ambiguity of the show was a mainstay of Xenophilia. Xena's gay cult following was turned on by the suggestive relationship she shared with female sidekick, Gabrielle. The two women were often seen tangled in a sensuous embrace that threatened to explode into unbridled passion. Female action heroes have come a long way since Wonder Woman made her first debut in *All-Star Comics* back in December of 1941.

FINDING THE MIDDLE

Xena was not a 'girls will be boys' woman like Demi Moore in

G.I .Jane. Demi played the role of the first woman trainee for the highly covert operations unit known as the Navy SEALS. When a superior officer (who thinks women have no place in combat) brutalizes her during an interrogation scene, Demi, dubbed 'Ramba', kicks the crap out of him and defiantly shouts, 'Suck my clit (click)!' Demi, sporting a buzz cut and buffed to the max, proved she could crawl like a man, shoot like a man, punch like a man, swear like a man and do one arm push ups like the best (and worst) of them.

After the release of *G.I. Jane*, Demi was interviewed by *Rolling Stone* magazine. 'Do you think things are worse for men now – that it's harder to be a straight white man . . . ?' Demi replied, ' . . . Maybe because the rules are changing and they're having to shift their understanding, they think so, but really, what's more difficult? It can only be more difficult if they're threatened by a woman who has some strength within herself. But if that's the case, then . . . deal with it.' When asked if she thought women being oppressed is a fact of life, Demi answered, 'Yes. That does exist. But I think it's changing, if only by the fact that we're sitting here now, talking about it – that it's a topic of discussion – that it's in a movie . . . maybe you have to go to the extreme to find the middle.'

Examples of the extreme are the *Lara Croft: Tomb Raider* movies that broke the $100-million-dollar box office records in 2001 and 2003 with voluptuous Angelina Jolie, playing the titanium kick-ass female action hero. Powerful, smart, independent, confident, sexy, rebellious. She's the goddess role model that women everywhere are worshipping and emulating. Stephanie Mencimer, an editor for the *Washington Monthly*, asks 'If men once lived vicariously through the escapades of John Rambo and Col. Matrix – in movies where women were mainly crime victims or in need of rescue – what does it mean when they love watching Lara Croft kick some bad-boy ass? It's a pretty sharp turn from misogyny to masochism.' For Mencimer, the dominatrix male-fantasy as an explanation for this shift doesn't cut it. Women are scratching their heads and wondering why is it that men suddenly don't seem to mind that women everywhere are kicking ass – women like tennis stars Venus and Serena Williams with their one hundred mile an hour serves and race car driver Milka Duno, who keeps butting into the lead? Hollywood's use of wires has allowed Angelina Jolie, Zhang Zi Yi, Lucy Liu and Cameron Diaz to annihilate their male rivals with flying jumps, high-kicks, jaw breaking punches and high speed whirls without developing the roped muscles of female body-builders. 'Men may have accepted women as action figures, but to achieve box-office success, the new action babes have to celebrate women's power without being so threatening that men would be afraid to sleep with the leading lady,' explains Mencimer. 'Women are still only allowed to be violent within certain parameters largely prescribed by what men are willing to tolerate.'

2

THE 'BOBBITT' SYNDROME

'The only time a woman really succeeds
in changing a man is when he's a baby.'
Natalie Wood

Even before the butt-kicking fumes disappeared behind Thelma
and Louise's airborne convertible, along came Lorena Bobbitt.
On 23 June 1993, after hacking off her husband's penis with
one foul swoop from an eight-inch carving knife, Lorena
Bobbitt told the police in broken English, 'He always have
orgasm and he doesn't wait for me to have orgasm. He's selfish.
It's not fair. So I pull back the sheets and then I did it.' Several
months later when Lorena was acquitted on the charge of
maliciously wounding her husband, the *Washington Post* reported
that 'women cheered and whooped brazenly', while men 'made
nervous jokes about sleeping on their stomachs.' Others
breathed a sigh of relief when a group calling itself the National
Feminist Association of Ecuador withdrew its pre-verdict threat
to castrate the first 100 American men they could get their
hands on.

The Lorena Bobbitt trial was preceded by the controversial
Anita Hill – Clarence Thomas sexual harassment hearings and
by the Mike Tyson and William Kennedy-Smith rape trials.
The public was totally pumped for a legendary battle of the

sexes and court TV delivered by providing gavel to gavel coverage. A Newsweek poll revealed that 60 per cent of the country was abuzz with the Bobbitt trial. Outside the Manassas, Virginia courthouse, 16 satellite up-link trucks and an army of 200 reporters were shoulder to shoulder with vendors who were selling white chocolates shaped like severed penises. Feminists, wearing 'Lorena Bobbitt for surgeon general' buttons, held up two fingers in a V for victory sign and made snipping gestures. T-shirts emblazoned with 'Love hurts' and 'Revenge – how sweet it is' were on sale with an optional autograph from John Wayne Bobbitt for an additional fee.

CNN carried the trial live in simulcast and doubled its ratings but when they made the faux pas of cutting away to the Russian summit, viewers were irate. Lorena Bobbitt had fulfilled every abused woman's fantasy and made every man's worst nightmare come true by committing the ultimate no-no in the battle of the sexes. In one primal swoop, Lorena shouted 'Enough!' for every woman who had ever been physically, sexually and emotionally abused by a male bully. The Bobbitt story with all its Freudian symbolism and gore, provoked passionate reactions and gender divisions. Men reacted as though Lorena was the commander-in-chief of a feminist guerrilla brigade. Women were either sharpening their steak knives or tripping over each other for fear they'd be labelled man haters. 'I can't believe people are getting so bent out of shape about this,' grumbled a trial watcher. 'Rapists are chopping off women's arms and getting out on parole two years later, and maybe it's covered once in the news. But let one woman touch one single penis and the whole country goes ballistic!' Why all the fuss over one amputated penis when the world is ho-hum about 80 million clitorises that have been ritually amputated by clitorectomy in Africa, Malasia, Indonesia and Sri Lanka? Both fascinated and repulsed at the same time, the public was hungry for details. What were the events leading up to the infamous deed and why did she do it?

FROM THE LAND OF VOLCANOES

Lorena Gallo, the eldest of three, was born in 1969 in Bucay, Ecuador near Volcan Cotopaxi, one of the tallest, angriest and most majestic active volcanoes in the world. Her father was a dental technician and typically 'the man of the house'. He traded their homeland of beauty for a homeland of opportunity and moved his family to the sprawling metropolis of Caracas, Venezuela. The Gallos were traditional Catholics who took their kids to church, movies, on hikes and picnics. Lorena was a big fan of *The Flintstones* on TV Venezuela. An early captive of the American dream, Lorena observed that, 'Even the Flintstones used to have microwaves – and they are middle class.'

In Venezuela, 15 years of age marks the transition from childhood into young adulthood. As a celebration gift, the Gallos bought 15-year-old Lorena a plane ticket to visit her cousins in a northern Virginia suburb of Washington DC. She arrived in the United States awestruck and starry eyed. 'I said to myself, "Oh my God, this is the place I want to be" . . . I feel like, oh, wow, this is like another planet . . . don't get me wrong . . . I love my country . . . I have patriotism. We do have McDonald's. We do have Pizza Hut. We do have hotels and beautiful shopping malls. But for some reason this is my dream in the back of my head.'

AMERICAN DREAMBOAT

In 1986, Lorena's mother travelled to Washington, DC. with

her children. Her father stayed behind and tried unsuccessfully to get a visa which meant the family had to return to Venezuela. Lorena begged her mother to let her stay. With her parents' blessing, Lorena remained in the United States, signed up for English immersion classes and got a job working as a nanny for the Castro family. In 1988, Mrs Castro invited Lorena to join her for an evening of fun at the Enlisted Marines Club. A handsome marine from Niagara Falls, New York, noticed Lorena across the crowded room. She was pretty and petite, personable and disarming, outgoing yet conventional and all of five feet two and 93 pounds. When he introduced himself, it was as though the uniformed male model on the Marine recruiting poster had magically come to life. John Wayne Bobbitt epitomized everything that was male and masculine. He flashed a manly smile, asked Lorena to dance and literally swept her off her feet. As the evening drew to a close, John told Lorena he wanted to see her again. He didn't have to twist her arm to get her phone number. He was saving the arm twisting for later.

After a ten month courtship, John popped the question as the love-struck couple sat across from each other eating decadent desserts in an ice cream parlour. Lorena popped the answer. Yes! Yes! Yes! 'I was in love with him. To me he represent everything. That was the beginning of starting my family here in the United States. And I feel that I wanted to have kids later on like a regular family. It was just like the beginning of my dream.'

Not unlike Forrest Gump, John Wayne Bobbitt struggled to keep up as a child and was placed in special education classes. Like Gump, he grew up to be smart enough for the Marines, patriotic enough to fight for corporate America, brave enough to kill on command and courageous enough to end up in a body bag if necessary. Even though John was intellectually challenged, it didn't pose a problem for his bride-to-be since neither John nor Lorena had a burning ambition to join the brainy Mensa Club any time soon.

It was a no frills wedding – no church, no bridesmaids, no flowers, no confetti, no fancy reception and no honeymoon vacation. 'Since we didn't have any money, I suggest just to go to the Justice of the Peaces. We both went there and we got married in Stafford on June eighteenth, 1989.'

The marriage started off on a sour note. John's younger cousin, Todd, moved into their small bachelor apartment and slept on the floor in the same room with them. Todd was like a younger brother to John. They'd both grown up together under the same roof. After John's alcoholic father ran out on his mother when John was four, his uncle and aunt took him in and raised him like their own son. Lorena complained about the lack of privacy. She didn't want to have sex with John while Todd was in the same room. But that wasn't the only reason she didn't want to have sex with John. John was one of those 'in and out' kind of guys. Lorena came to the conclusion that 'Well, maybe this is it when you're married.'

After only one month of marriage, Lorena was already bored, lonely and fed up. Returning home to an empty apartment after working all day as a manicurist at a nail sculpting salon wasn't Lorena's idea of marital bliss. John was out almost every night until the wee hours of the morning getting tanked with cousin Todd. Lorena finally coaxed John and Todd to let her tag along with them on one of their boys' nights out. While driving home after a night on the town, John started speeding and honking and zigzagging all over the freeway. 'Oh my God, we're going to crash!' Lorena shrieked. 'That's when he hit me for the first time. He punched me . . . I was crying the whole time.'

John was still steaming mad when they got back to the apartment. Todd waited outside while John hustled Lorena inside. 'He grabbed my hair and slapped me, he kicked me to the wall . . . he kept slapping me.' When a security guard showed up at the door to investigate the noise, John said, 'We had an argument. A little discussion.' The guard asked if they were married and John answered, 'Yeah, we're married. We're just having a little discussion like husband and wife.' Then the guard asked Lorena if she had a place to go and she answered, 'No, but I leave anyways.' Lorena left the apartment and drove to her employer's nail sculpting salon. She parked outside and slept in the car.

The living situation with Todd got worse but John refused to kick him out. 'He was going out drinking with Todd and sometimes they come back later at night,' Lorena recalls. 'And I guess he had too much to drink so he had to vomitate. And so he did it in the closet. And he expected me to clean. So, I said no, I don't want to clean that because it's dirty. And I just took my shoes. He vomitated on my shoes and I had to clean my own shoes, but I didn't clean the rest. So, he grabbed me by my hair. He punched me again. He kicked me and slapped me.' The Marine Corps started assigning John extra duty and fining him for coming in late.

Lorena discovered that Todd had a drug problem when she found tarnished spoons and syringes in the apartment. She phoned John's aunt in Niagara Falls and informed her that her son, Todd, had a drug problem. Without notice, John's aunt, uncle and cousins arrived on the doorstep at Thanksgiving and announced they were staying for a one-week visit. 'I had no idea they were coming. I wasn't prepared.' Lorena offered to help them rent a room somewhere else. They declined.

UNHOLY NIGHT

After Thanksgiving, Todd checked out of the apartment and out of their lives. John found a two-bedroom apartment and informed Lorena they were moving. Lorena was looking forward to being alone with her new husband and celebrating their first Christmas together. A fight broke out over the Christmas tree. Lorena wanted a plastic one that they could re-use. John wanted a real one. 'He started to torture me. He started using some technique that he teaches the Marines. That hurt a lot because my arm was twisted. He was just hitting me. Hitting me in my chest, my arms.'

Lorena learned she was pregnant in the spring of 1990 and convinced herself that the pregnancy would bring John closer to her and put an end to the abuse. 'I bought a little bib, and I wanted to surprise him, so I put the little bib in his chest and he took it off. "What is this?"' he asked. Lorena looked at him quizzically, 'That doesn't mean anything to you?' John was furious with her for getting 'fucking pregnant'. He started thumbing through the Yellow Pages searching for a list of abortion clinics. 'He was saying that the baby would look ugly, and he also was saying that I'm not going to be a good mother.' When Lorena refused to abort the baby, John told her he was going to leave her. 'I was crying and crying . . . I didn't want to have a baby without a father. I didn't grow up like that.' John escorted Lorena to an abortion clinic. 'I couldn't realize that I was doing this. We both went there and he was really making me scared. He said the needles are going to be big and I was going to die . . . I was hysterical, crying and the nurse said,

'What's going on here?' She took me to a room to calm me down.' The baby was aborted on 15 June 1990.

Janna Buscutti owned the nail-sculpting salon where Lorena worked as a manicurist. Janna was more than just Lorena's employer. She was a friend, a confidante and a surrogate mother. When Lorena confided to Janna about John's abuse, Janna confronted him about it. 'She nags and I get frustrated,' John complained with a shrug. Janna's husband sat John down for a man-to-man talk but John was unrepentant. The abuse continued and Janna advised Lorena to get out of the marriage before things got worse.

By the summer of 1990, instead of getting a divorce, Lorena and John bought a white rambler 'Ozzie and Harriet' house on Pine Street in Manassas. Lorena wanted a townhouse but 'John didn't want townhouses because he said one wall belongs to another family.' Even though they couldn't afford the house on Pine, John insisted he needed a big garage. Lorena gave in. She was counting on John's bi-weekly check from the Marines to help her with the payments.

WAR OF THE ROSES

John was looking less and less like a Marine poster boy and more and more like the Terminator as he turned the house on Pine into a house of horrors. Using Marine Corps head butts, karate kicks and choke holds, John pretended he was karate man, Jean-Claude Van Damme. He'd drag Lorena across the floor by the hair and read aloud from a book called *How To Satisfy Your Wife and Have Her Beg For More*. 'Every time I locked myself in the bathroom or in the bedroom he will punch the door and come with a screwdriver . . . and unscrew the knobs of the doors,' recalled Lorena. The Marine Corps assigned

John to an abuse counsellor after Lorena filed a complaint accusing him of intentionally backing into her with an open car door and knocking her to the ground.

BATTERED HUSBAND

In January, 1991, John took terminal leave from the Marine Corps. He was charged with assault and battery one month later, entered a plea of guilty, then filed a counter-complaint that his wife kicked him in the groin. He accused her of being a husband batterer who jumped on him, swung at him, kicked and punched him, ranted and raved, nagged and complained. 'It's not proper for a lady to strike out in such a way just because things aren't going well,' John told the judge. He swore he never abused Lorena – just restrained her. The court dropped the charges arising from both complaints.

Over the next two years, John held 19 different jobs including cabbie, Red Lobster cashier and nightclub bouncer. Lorena kept her job at the nail salon and continued to be John's meal ticket and punching bag. He started seeing other women and bragging about his affairs as he showed her lists of the women he'd slept with. He even asked her to supply gas money for one of his dates.

During one of their frequent arguments, John raped Lorena for the first time. She turned to a neighbour, Ken Willoughby, for help. Ken was a pastor and tried to counsel John but John was unresponsive and the violence escalated. One night when Lorena had the TV turned up too loud, John forced her to have anal sex with him. 'He grabbed and he turned me . . . and I was with my stomach down and he did it. I was bleeding.' Whenever they had sex after that, John threatened to sodomize her. 'He told me forced sex excited him,' Lorena later testified in court under cross-examination, 'I remember every time he had the anal sex with me. He hurt me . . . Maybe you don't understand because you're a man. But it hurt me.' Lorena learned from her cultural background that a woman is responsible when her marriage fails. Lorena blamed herself for the abuse and felt unworthy of John's love. He convinced her that no man would ever treat her well, that she was skinny and ugly and had a bad figure, that her breasts were too small and her butt was too big. He joked about her English and her race and threatened to have her deported. John's unrelenting criticism took a toll on Lorena's self-esteem. She felt ugly and undesirable. 'He always said I wasn't going to have anybody. I thought, maybe this guy is right. I'm not going to have anybody. He always said men was going to treat me so bad and I didn't deserve anybody. I always remember those things. I was scared to meet somebody else . . . I feel like maybe I have to please him.'

Lorena wasn't getting any help with the bills as John drifted from job to job. In desperation, she began stealing products from the nail salon and planned to start her own business sculpting nails on the side for some extra money. One day, she showed the stolen products to John and said, 'I stole these products for you.' John hauled Lorena over to Janna's place and made her confess. Lorena was apologetic and sobbed, 'I feel like I wanted to do something. I cannot buy food, cannot pay the mortgage payment, or utilities.' Lorena neglected to tell her employer that she also embezzled $7,200 from the salon. Janna later checked her books and discovered the discrepancy. Instead of pressing charges, she docked Lorena's commissions.

In spite of her financial problems, Lorena somehow managed to afford a new satellite dish, two cars, a computer for John and expensive new dresses for herself. When she got picked up for shoplifting, she explained, 'I thought maybe if I dressed up, maybe he [John] doesn't see another woman.' The courts assigned her community work.

The house on Pine went into foreclosure and the cars were repossessed. Faced with financial ruin and the collapse of her marriage, Lorena found herself right back where she started – at Mrs Castro's house in Stafford. She flashed back to her childhood and to an episode of *The Flintstones* about finding the pot of gold at the end of the rainbow. Instead of gold, Lorena found 'bedrock'.

In September, 1992, John came to visit Lorena at Mrs Castro's house after a one year separation. 'He told me he's never going to hit me again. That he will be a nice guy and he will respect me like a wife . . . He also told me that he loved me and I believe him . . . and he tell me he's going to work hard and everything.' Lorena was worried about AIDS because of John's womanizing. She asked him to get tested and he agreed. The results came back negative 'so, I accept my husband back.' John landed a job at Burger King.

In April, 1993, Lorena and John moved to an apartment in Maplewood Park with a view of a strip mall and a discount grocery store. When John lost his job at the Burger King, his behaviour turned ugly again. Lorena decided to file for divorce but she needed proof of the abuse. She bought a tape recorder and concealed it in her purse so that she could capture the abuse on tape. John found the tape recorder and flew into a rage. After destroying the tape, he slammed Lorena up against a wall, booted her in the stomach, pulled her hair and slapped her around before raping her and fleeing with scratch marks on his face.

'I couldn't sleep. I couldn't eat. People were complaining about my work . . . on many occasions, I would just leave my work and go to the bathroom and start to cry. My body start to speaking. I'm a good nail technician and I never have problems, but this started affecting me.' Lorena saw a doctor and was referred to an abuse hot-line and advised to get a restraining order against John. Lorena quickly collected some boxes together and began packing her things.

John agreed to a divorce but he told Lorena that divorced or not, he would stalk her, find her and force her to have sex with him whenever he wanted. On Monday, 21 June, Lorena went to the Prince William Court House and talked to court counsellor, Steven Rogue. She asked him about getting a restraining order against her husband. A neighbour encouraged her to stay in a women's shelter that night but Lorena stayed at the apartment because John's friend, Robbie Johnson, was visiting at the time and she felt safe with Robbie there.

Lorena spent the evening of 23 June 1993, with a neighbour, then grabbed a snack at KFC and went home. She crawled into bed wearing spandex shorts and a T-shirt and fell asleep. Between three and three-thirty a.m., she was awakened by the slam of the apartment door. John had been out on the town bar hopping and knocking back beers and B-52s with his friend, Robbie Johnson. After helping Robbie make up a bed on the pull-out couch in the living room, John staggered into the bedroom, stripped naked and climbed into bed next to Lorena.

JOHN'S VERSION

'I was too exhausted to like, get up to perform. But I wanted to. I rolled over and I was on top of her. And then I just remember that she put her knees up, and she put her arms around me, and then I just fell back off to sleep. And I don't remember anything else happening after that, until I was just laying on my back. I mean – then at that point I opened my eyes because I seen her sitting on my side, like checking me and seeing if I was able to perform for her . . . after that I just closed my eyes and went to sleep because I couldn't even – I couldn't stay awake, I was too exhausted. The next thing I remember is she was sitting on my left side again. I woke up a little, I opened my eyes just barely. I just noticed what she was doing, just sitting there . . .'

LORENA'S VERSION

'The next thing I remember, he was on top of me. I said, "No, get off of me. I don't want to have sex" and he wouldn't get off of me . . . and he grabbed my wrists and press it down to my hips. Then he – I felt like I couldn't breathe, and he was – his chest and his right shoulder, was on my face and my mouth. And then he – I asked him, "What are you doing?" and he didn't say anything. I said, "I don't want to have sex", and he wouldn't listen to me. He wouldn't let me go, and he started to pull down my underwears with his foot . . . I was fighting and I just grabbed my pants . . . I heard my underwear rip. And his chest was really on me. And he's heavy. I couldn't breath, I couldn't scream . . . I couldn't even move . . . He opened my legs and he put his tongue inside (my throat), very, very low . . . I felt like I was going to throw up . . . He continued doing it, having intercourse . . . I felt like my vagina was ripping up . . . he pushed me away. And I was crying. I stand up. And I said, "why you do this to me?" He pushed me away and said, "Leave me alone" . . . so I stood up from the bed and I was just looking for my pants. I put my spandex shorts on and I said, "you can't do this to me. And you did it again and again and again . . . why do you do this to me?" And then he said he doesn't care, and he said "leave me alone". I cry and I cry.'

Lorena went to the kitchen for a drink of water. 'I feel trapped. I don't know where to go. I don't know what to do. I was very scared of him. I didn't want him to rape me any more. I didn't want him to hit me any more. I did not want him to follow me and rape me . . . The refrigerator light was on . . . the door was really wide open . . . I was scared . . . I was physically hurt. I was feeling hurt. I don't know. It was everything together . . . I couldn't describe it'. Lorena turned and the first thing she saw was a knife – a red handled eight-inch filet knife.

'I grabbed that knife and I went to the bedroom and, and he was there . . . and he kind of, like, moved or something. I don't know . . . I remember many things. I was thinking the first time he hit me. I was thinking the first time he raped me . . . I remember every time that he had anal sex with me. It hurt me, it hurt . . . I was thinking so many things, really quick . . . I don't know . . . I just wanted him to disappear. I just wanted him to leave me alone, to leave my life alone. I don't want to see him any more . . . and I took the sheets off and I cut him.'

JOHN'S VERSION

' . . . She pulled on my groin area twice, I think. I felt a couple of jerks. And then after that she just cut it off . . . I just sprang up like I wanted to, you know, scream but there was nothing there. I was bleeding and she just . . . it hurt real bad . . . I thought she just, you know, grabbed it and just pulled it right off my body. I didn't see a knife. I didn't see nothing. I just sat up real quick, like I was in real pain, a lot of pain. And I held myself. I was bleeding. I was confused. I was like hysterical . . . I just caught her out of the corner of my eye just dashing out of the bedroom. And after she did it she gave like a – she gave

31

it a grunt like when she did it and just ran . . . I felt dizzy. I felt like, you know, weird. But then I collected myself. I knew I had to get some help.'

LORENA'S VERSION

Lorena managed to hook her purse over her arm as she dashed out of the apartment door in a panic, knife in one hand, two-thirds of a severed penis in the other. Next thing Lorena knew she was in her 1991 Mercury Capri approaching the inter-section of Old Centerville and Maplewood streets. 'I drove and I drove really quick . . . I tried to turn but I couldn't because my – my hands were busy, and I just scream and I saw it, and I throw it out . . . I throw that away.' John's penis flew out the car window and landed in the tall grass in an empty lot by the Patty-Kake Day Care Center.

'I just wanted to see Janna. I never really have this kind of sensation. I just drove really fast and I wanted to see her. I stop at the Nail Sculpture shop, maybe thinking she was there or something . . . Nobody was there. Nobody was there, so I – I just keep on crying and screaming . . . I couldn't open the door 'cause I have a knife in my right hand. So I throw that in the trash can. I wanted to grab the phone, but then I saw a little blood in my hand. I ran out and then I fell and really quickly stand up and I went in and I washed my hands. And I washed my hands really quickly and I dial the phone.' Janna's telephone answering machine intercepted Lorena's call, so Lorena drove over to Janna's house. She pounded on the door. Janna opened the door, took one look at Lorena's ghostly face and her first thoughts were, 'Oh my God, what has John done to her now?' Lorena told Janna that she threw John's 'thingie' out the car window.

JOHN'S VERSION

John was bleeding profusely and holding both hands over his amputated groin area. He woke up his house guest and said, 'Robbie, you have to take me to the hospital.' Robbie saw the blood dripping from John's groin and gasped, 'Oh, my God.'

John and Robbie arrived at the Prince William hospital emergency room at 5.03 a.m. John had a bloody sheet wrapped around his hand which was covering his groin. Dr Steven Sharpe asked to see what he assumed was an injured hand. 'That's not where I'm cut,' John said as he pulled down his pants and showed the doctor his stub. 'And he like kind of stepped back, you know like "wow." Then he got an orderly to put me on a table and apply pressure . . . '

Dr Sharpe quickly summoned Dr James Sehn, the on-call urologist who arrived at about 6 a.m. 'It was a horrific sight,' said Dr Sehn. 'He was on his back and there was just a clot (stump) left where there should have been a penis. The medical staff were surprised he hadn't bled to death. They told John he'd have to learn to pee like the other fifty percent of the population.' '. . . At that time, you know, there was nothing they could do, just close it up, you know, I wouldn't be normal any more. I'd have to sit down to urinate,' John recalled.

MEANWHILE . . .

Lorena contacted the police and told them John's penis was somewhere near the Patty-Kake Day Care Center. Police officers were already at the Bobbitt apartment searching for the missing part. A dispatcher sent rescue personnel armed with flashlights to the Day Care Center on a treasure hunt. Volunteer fireman Michael Perry spotted the treasure first. He stuck it in a Ziploc bag, then wrapped it in ice. The penis was rushed to the hospital. Eight to nine hours had passed since the time of the amputation. John Bobbitt was quickly wheeled into the O.R. for re-attachment surgery.

While John was under the knife for the second time, Lorena was undergoing forensic tests to prove that John had raped her. She then went to Prince William police headquarters and made a statement. She told Detective Peter Weintz about the rape and that John pushed her away afterwards. 'Sometimes he just push me away, make me feel really bad because that's not fair, that's not nice . . . He always have orgasm and he doesn't wait for me to have orgasm. He's selfish. I don't think it's fair, so I pull back the sheets and then I did it.'

THE RES-ERECTION

In an historical nine-and-a-half-hour microsurgery operation, Dr Sehn and a team of skilled surgeons successfully re-attached John's penis into a working organ again. Millions of viewers briefly glimpsed at a colour photo of the severed penis on their TV screens. Christine Sehn, wife of the famous surgeon who resurrected John's penis, said that she was hounded by angry women who wished her husband hadn't done it, who wished Lorena had flushed the little extraterrestrial down the toilet or stuffed it in the Cuisinart.

Anthropologist, Helen Fisher of New York's Museum of Natural History was surprised the big 'no-no' hadn't happened more often considering the high incidence of violence between the sexes. Cutting off penises in the USA is uncommon but that's not the custom everywhere. Fred Graham's guest on Court TV claimed that dismemberment in South America is not so infrequent. Cultural differences are also prevalent in Thailand where according to a 1995 article in a medical journal, about 100 women in the 1970s severed the penises of their philandering husbands while they were asleep. Reattachments were tried on 18 cases but mostly with poor results. In 1992, in Brampton, Ontario, a 48-year-old woman cut off her husband's penis but was acquitted on the grounds that she was a battered woman. In 1997, Kim Tran, a 38-year-old woman from Vancouver, Canada, cut off her sleeping husband's penis with a meat cleaver and flushed it down the toilet. She found out he was having an affair with a younger woman and pleaded with him to stop. 'I begged him but he wouldn't listen,' she said. Tran pleaded guilty to aggravated assault and received a two-year conditional sentence with no jail time.

THE VERDICT

Lorena Bobbitt was staring at a 20-year prison term and deportation for disarming her husband of his sexual weapon. With millions of viewers glued to their court TV screens, Lorena took the stand. Wearing a navy and white Sunday school dress and a small cross around her neck, Lorena sniffled and sobbed as she described her four year 'marital Armageddon' – the anal rapes, the Kung Fu chops, the insults, the punching, shoving, slapping, dragging, kicking, choking and even the time John vomited on her shoes.

The prosecution argued that Lorena was sexually demanding, obsessively possessive and a battering wife who amputated her sleeping husband's penis out of anger and revenge. Connie James, the wife of another marine, testified that Lorena once told her that if she caught her husband cheating on her, 'I would cut his dick off because that would hurt him more than just killing him.'

When John took the stand, he described scenes from a different marriage. Lorena's defense attorney, James Lowe, caught the handsome ex-marine in a 'string of outrageous lies'. Even John's drinking buddies took the stand and admitted that John bragged about how much he liked forced sex and liked to make women cry, scream and bleed. One by one, witnesses paraded before the jury confirming John's brutality and reign of terror. Psychiatrists for both sides agreed that Lorena suffered from post-traumatic stress syndrome caused by John's unrelenting abuse during their four-year marriage and that she retaliated in a state of trauma. Dr Susan Feister called Lorena a 'typical battered woman. Brutalized repeatedly, she attacked the weapon which was the instrument of her torture – that is her husband's penis.' Attorney Blair Howard called it a classic case of 'irresistible impulse'.

John watched the last day of the trial on TV. After seven hours of deliberation, a jury of five men and seven women delivered the verdict to a pin-drop quiet courtroom. Lorena Bobbitt was found not guilty and acquitted by reason of temporary insanity for what the law called malicious wounding of her husband. When the verdict came down, Lorena didn't know how to react. 'Is that good?' she asked her attorney as they whisked her off to Virginia's State mental hospital for a 45-day period of psychiatric evaluation. John had already been tried earlier on a marital rape charge but was acquitted even though Lorena's defense team presented evidence of cruelty and abuse. John Wayne Bobbitt symbolized the drunk and abusing husbands of the world that women wanted to 'get even' with.

THE AFTERMATH
Lorena Bobbitt was crowned America's 'tabloid celebrity of the month'. She became a feminist icon, national folk heroine, freedom fighter and a martyr-heroine-saint role model. After her

acquittal, even Lorena began to fancy her new image. Feminists made her into a poster girl for their campaign to end sexual violence against women.

Patricia Ireland, President of the National Organization of Women (NOW), appeared on Larry King Live welcoming the Bobbitt verdict and using it as an occasion for promoting the passage of the federal Violence Against Women Act. Lorena's aggressiveness was heralded as an example of a new grass roots militancy. The common consensus was that Lorena Bobbitt had gotten away with a crime that men had been getting away with for centuries. John Wayne Bobbitt got what he deserved.

Complaints were voiced about the deterioration of standards of accountability and the return of 'an eye for an eye' justice.

'Sexual mutilation is an act of hatred or revenge,' wrote Wendy Kaminer, author of *I'm Dysfunctional, You're Dysfunctional*. 'Unlike many battered wives, she (Lorena) seemed motivated more by rage than fear . . . Lorena Bobbitt could hardly claim to have been protecting herself from her (sleeping) husband when she took a knife to him. Her actions were more likely to escalate conflict than resolve it. Cutting off a man's penis as someone said, "tends to piss a guy off".' Kaminer charged that, 'if Lorena Bobbitt was innocent of intentionally dismembering her husband then a large majority of people in prison should probably go free. Violent offenders often have trouble resisting their impulses – that's what makes them violent. They often have histories of deprivation and abuse and were raised in environments in which violence was a primary form of self expression. They have good reason to be crazy, at least temporarily, and many may have had a more credible insanity defense than the one successfully raised by Lorena Bobbitt.'

IN THE MEN'S CORNER

Rush Limbaugh, in a *Newsweek* article, No Tears For Lorena, shook his finger at America and said, 'Shame on feminists for backing her, and damn us all for watching . . . let's face it – John and Lorena Bobbitt are losers', and 'Those who view all men as potential rapists – have made Lorena into a symbol of the plight of battered women'. They claim she mutilated her husband in self defense. Or, in the penetrating phrase of her attorney, 'A life is more valuable than a penis.' 'I would add that a life such as John Bobbitt's is more valuable with a penis.'

'At least she left him his balls' wrote a reporter for the *Nation.*

'It's going to be really hard for either of them to get a date,' said Tonight Show host, Jay Leno.

David Kaplan of *Newsweek* predicted that men would be 'less likely to insist that women belonged in the kitchen.'

John Bobbitt, after learning that he would regain full sexual function and after being offered over a million dollars to star in a porno film declared, 'This is the best thing that ever happened to me.'

IN THE WOMEN'S CORNER

'If a fellow insists on using his penis as a weapon, I say that one way or another, he ought to be swiftly disarmed', declared Barbara Ehrenreich who compared Lorena Bobbitt to a 'warrior woman' in the tradition of 'Thelma and Louise'.

It's 'an act of revolution', wrote Camille Paglia. 'It's kind of like the Boston Tea Party. It's a wake-up call . . . it has to send a chill through every man in the world.'

Feminist author, Naomi Wolfe, and other women who were sick and tired of hearing about victim feminism felt it was time to stop whining and go for the power. Men are not, repeat <u>not</u>, the enemy.

After the trial, Lorena announced, 'I can't ever imagine dating another man'. Except for those contemplating a sex change, few men can ever imagine dating her either.

BOBBITT SYNDROME – A CURE

Lorena got off. She got off – not in the bedroom but in the courtroom. If she'd been getting off in the bedroom, the whole gory nightmare might have been avoided. 'He always have orgasm and doesn't wait for me', complained Lorena after the fact. 'He's selfish. It's not fair. So I pull back the sheets and then I did it.' Lorena's famous words still echo hauntingly in the minds of the guilty who suffer from castration anxiety and insomnia ever since the well publicized amputation. Shere Hite's best selling book, *The Hite Report*, offers a cure for sufferers of Post-Traumatic Bobbitt Syndrome by teaching three basic facts about female sexuality and anatomy:

1. WOMEN'S SEX ORGANS ARE AS BIG AS MEN'S

The clitoral system is as 'large' and as 'responsive' as the male penis and responds to sexual stimulation the same way a penis does. Australian urology surgeon, Dr Helen O'Connell, discovered that the clitoris is twice as big as its depiction in the medical anatomy books used by doctors and surgeons. 'Sometimes the whole structure is drawn as a dot . . . They draw the tip of the iceberg but not the iceberg', reports Dr O'Connell who is re-mapping female genitalia and researching the blood vessels and nerves that cause the clitoris to swell and engorge in much the same way the penis does in men. The clitoris extends up to three and a half inches into a woman's body in a pyramid of tissue whose sole function is to give sexual pleasure, reports O'Connell in the Journal of Urology. Sigmund Freud's mistaken belief that clitoral orgasms are a sign of less maturity in women than vaginal orgasms has prejudiced and misinformed generations of women about how they function sexually. An orgasm is an orgasm. Like a sneeze, it can be big or small.

2. WOMEN GET ERECTIONS

Famed sexual researcher, Alfred Kinsey, concluded that sexual arousal occurs through the same mechanism for both men and women. Blood flows to the genitals during sexual arousal where it gets trapped – leading to an erect penis in men and an erect clitoris and a lubricated vagina in women. Female sex organs, although internal and not so visible, expand during arousal to approximately the same volume as an erect penis. In short, the only real difference between men's and women's erections is that men's are on the outside of their bodies and women's are, for the most part, on the inside. Dr Irwin Goldstein, a urologist with the Boston University Medical School, published a paper with a research team showing that the enzyme upon which the Viagra drug works its magic exists in the smooth muscles of the clitoris as well as the penis.

3. CLITORAL STIMULATION EVOKES ORGASM

Just like stimulation of the tip of the male penis evokes male orgasm which takes place inside the lower body of the male, stimulation of the clitoris evokes female orgasm which takes place deeper in the body around the vagina and other structures. For many women, clitoral stimulation is not 'foreplay' leading to 'the big event' of intercourse. Clitoral stimulation *is* the big event. The Janus Report On Sexual Behaviour which claims to be the first scientific national survey since the Kinsey Report, reveals that 16 per cent of the women surveyed rarely or never achieved orgasm (22 per cent for women not employed outside the home, ten per cent for women with a full time outside career). Another ten per cent of women described their honeymoon as boring and nine per cent thought that it was traumatic. Eighty-nine per cent of women and 82 per cent of men thought the battle of the sexes still existed today. Twenty-eight per cent of men and 17 per cent of women reported 'sex' and 'extramarital affairs' as the primary reason for divorce. In 1994, the Social Organization of Sexuality conducted a broad-based study documenting Americans' sexual lives and found that 34 per cent of women lacked interest in sex (compared with ten per cent of men), 22 per cent got no pleasure from sex (about eight per cent for men) and 25 per cent of women were unable to achieve orgasm (about eight per cent for men).

President Clinton claimed he never had sex with 'that woman' Ms Lewinsky, because sex equals intercourse – which may explain why 'that woman' kept coming back for more. In spite of the information revolution, the prehistoric view of sex and of the vagina as a receptacle for the penis is alive and well. Commonly used slang words describing the sex act continue to perpetuate the polarizing notion of the aggressive male and the passive female. Men fuck. Women get fucked. Men cruise. Women get cruised. Men are on the make. Women get made. Men ball and score. Women get balled, humped, jumped and thumped. These slang expressions imply that sex equals pene-tration. A man's penis is a cock, dick, prick, rod, bone, pecker, willy. A woman's clitoris (which is the key source of female sexual pleasure) has few slang words for referencing it. 'Cunt', 'pussy' and 'box' somehow miss the mark.

41

EPILOGUE

Since the verdicts and the divorce, the 'not guilty' tabloiders were back in the courtroom again. John Bobbitt served 12 days in jail in 1994 for battery of his new fiancée. That same year, he reconstituted his damaged manhood by starring in a porno film called *Uncut* based on his own true story for which he was paid over a million dollars. One year later, he settled a paternity suit claim that was lodged by another woman. After starring in a second porno film with endless scenes of heterosexual intercourse and 'cum' shots and after posing naked for *GQ* magazine next to an article called 'Forrest Stump', John saw the light, found Jesus and became a man of the cloth. As an ordained minister of the Universal Life Church, John oversaw baptisms, weddings and funerals and prayed a lot as he searched for a site in Las Vegas for his congregation. When a reporter asked him what he intended to call his congregation, John smiled and replied, 'John Wayne Bobbitt's Church Without An Organ.' By age 30, John concluded that serving God was an unfulfilling career choice, so he swapped his preaching job for a 'ranch hand' job at the Moonlight Bunny Ranch near Carson City, Nevada – home of 20 working prostitutes. John's duties at the legal brothel included greeting the 'johns', running errands, driving the limo and bartending. His porn movies which grossed $30 million between 1994 and 1997 became popular gift shop items at the ranch.

A Nevada newspaper reported that John is still in love with the woman who chopped off his manhood in 1993. 'I should never have left her', said John, nostalgically. 'You don't know what you've got until you lose it.'

Lorena Gallo, now using her maiden name, has remained single and is living with her parents. In December 1997, she was back in a Virginia courtroom charged with punching her mother in the face. With no book or movie deals from Hollywood's phallic power brokers, Lorena has drifted into obscurity. Unlike John, Lorena wasn't offered any starring roles in pornographic movies – presumably because her breasts were too small or her hips were too big or because a title like *Lorena For Surgeon General, Petty Larceny* or *Butcher Wife* might turn guys off.

3

LOVE, RAPE AND
MARY LETOURNEAU

'The only men who are too young
are the ones who write their love
letters in crayon, wear pyjamas with
feet or fly for half fare'
Phyllis Diller

Rape stories usually begin as 'whodunits' but when the
'whodunit' turns out to be a 'she-dunit' instead of a 'he-dunit',
the media calls it a 'whydunit'. Why would an attractive
woman with a husband, four kids, a house and a successful
teaching career, risk it all for a pubescent boy with peach fuzz?

He was 12 years old – a shy, dark skinned Samoan-American
with almond shaped eyes and jet black hair. She was his sixth-
grade teacher at Shorewood Elementary school in Burien,
Washington – a petite, 36-year-old, fair-skinned blond, with a
warm smile and a sunny disposition. Mary Kay Letourneau's
relationship with Vili Fualaau began in 1991 when Vili was in
her second-grade class. 'I was six or seven. She encouraged me
in my drawing. She bought me art supplies and took me to art
classes and museums,' recalled Vili. Mary helped her 'Warhol
protégé' get scholarships for Saturday art classes at a local
community college. She also tutored and guided his literary

talents and by the age of 12, Vili was already writing poetry with the wisdom of a Zen master. 'There was a respect, an insight, a spirit, an understanding between us that grew over time,' explained Mary. 'The kind of feeling you have with a brother or sister – a feeling that they're part of your life forever . . . I didn't know what it meant . . . I felt that one day he might marry my daughter.'

Like other boys in Mrs Letourneau's class, Vili fantasized about hugging and kissing her, about squeezing her breasts and making passionate love to her, but never in his wildest dreams did he think they'd ever really get naked together and do 'the wild thing'. Mrs Letourneau was a married woman. Mrs Letourneau was one year younger than his own mother. Mrs Letourneau's son, Steve Jr, was Vili's age.

UNLIKELY TRIANGLE

Some women are so fertile, they can get pregnant just looking at a guy. In the early eighties, a macho football player named Steve Letourneau caught Mary's eye at an Arizona State University frat party. She got pregnant. After agonizing over what to do about the unwanted pregnancy, Mary opted for an abortion even though it was against her Catholic upbringing. Three months later, she was pregnant again with Steve. This time, Mary opted to do the right Catholic thing and chose a shotgun wedding instead of an abortion.

The newlyweds moved to the land of the midnight sun, where Steve's parents lived. Alaska. Steve landed a job there as a cargo loading specialist (moving baggage) with Alaska Airlines and soon got transferred to Seattle. In spite of some early turbulence, the couple decided they were together for the long haul and fastened their seat belts. Four children later

(Steve Jr, Mary Claire, Nicholas and Jacqueline), they moved to a modest house in the middle-class suburb of Normandy Park where their kids could grow up surrounded by tall evergreens and watch pastel sunsets over Puget Sound. According to a neighbour, the Letourneaus appeared to be the 'picture-perfect family'.

Steve worked odd hours and Mary was left with the lion's share of responsibility raising four kids. She eventually got a teaching job at Shorewood elementary school where she earned a reputation as a brilliant and devoted teacher. By the early 1990s, Mary and Steve's debts outperformed their double incomes and a posse of creditors galloped in for the kill. In May, 1994, the Letourneau's filed for Chapter 13 bankruptcy. Mary's inner circle of friends knew the marriage was in trouble when the couple stopped being publicly civil to each other. 'He had a girlfriend then . . . and I was well aware of that,' Mary conceded. When she asked Steve for a divorce, he reminded her of their wedding vow 'til death do us part'. He vowed when he married her that, come hell or high water, he'd never get divorced because his parents got divorced and he wasn't going to suffer the same fate. In October 1995, Mary received some devastating news. Her beloved father, John Schmitz, had terminal cancer. Instead of offering sympathy, Steve barked, 'What do you want me to do?' Adding insult to injury, Mary suffered a miscarriage a few months later and was teetering on a nervous breakdown. With no one to turn to, she took comfort in her mentor relationship with her sixth grade student, Vili Fualaau.

ROBBING THE CRADLE

Indian summer came and went and the weatherman settled in to an easy job predicting the Seattle weather for the next six months with perfect accuracy . . . rain, rain, rain. The dark and stormy months were hardly noticeable as Mary and her young protégé worked on school projects together at her home. Mary started inviting the boy for sleepovers and included him in family outings while his mother, Soona, worked the night shift in a pastry factory. Soona, an immigrant from Western Samoa, got suspicious about her son's unusually close friendship with his middle-aged teacher and questioned him about it. 'He said there was nothing between them and I assumed I could trust her with my son.'

It happened in the spring of 1996. Vili was 12 going on 13. He had a slender build like Leonardo DiCaprio, a deepened voice and had already surpassed Mary in height. She was flattered by his flirtatious comments, his love poems and the music tapes he recorded for her. Mariah Carey and Celine Dion said it all. 'Even before we kissed, I'd been feeling closer to Mary . . . It took me a while to build up my courage, but one day I brought up the subject. I told Mary I wanted to make love to her . . . At first it scared her. She tried to discourage me and even wrote me a letter saying that someday I'd grow up and fall in love with a girl my own age. But I told her, "You're the woman I want."' To commemorate his upcoming thirteenth birthday, Vili slipped a silver ring onto Mary's finger and kissed her awkwardly. 'Her lips were so warm and sweet. She was so beautiful, I couldn't believe this was happening. She was the mom of kids I used to play with. I was excited and scared all at the same time.' Mary responded to the boy's inexperienced kiss. 'That was the turning point when maybe I shouldn't have responded, but I did.' Vili asked Mary to have sex with him. When Mary graciously declined, Vili didn't give up. There was always a next time.

LIKE ROSE AND JACK

It happened for the very first time a few days prior to Vili's thirteenth birthday. Vili, who was a regular guest at the Letourneau house, appeared to be asleep on the couch as Steve left for work. Mary got up to lock the door behind her husband and when she turned around, Vili was there. 'He held his arms out and pulled me towards him. In a few seconds, my life had turned over.' Mary could feel Vili's erection pressed against her. She wanted to help him, to relieve his sexual tension 'so he would not have those feelings'. She went down on the boy and as she put her mouth on his penis, he climaxed almost immediately. That was 'the beginning of the end', Mary recalls. The flood gates that had damned their smoldering passion burst wide open and they found themselves swept away in each other's arms, tumbling down onto the couch with Vili on top pushing himself against her. Throwing caution to the wind, Mary allowed herself to desire him as badly as he desired her. In the magic of the moment, she allowed him to enter her. It was Vili's first time and in a way it was Mary's first time, too. She'd never felt this way about anyone before. At 36, she'd found the man of her dreams – creative, sensitive, shy, passionately romantic and . . . 12 years old.

On 19 June, 1996, Vili had been working late on an art project with Mary at the Letourneau house. While he was cleaning up afterwards, a fight broke out between Mary and Steve. It wasn't the first time Vili had witnessed the mud slinging couple hurling threats and insults at each other. Vili bolted off into the night and headed for home but Mary chased after him in the minivan and picked him up.

They drove to a secluded parking lot in the suburb of Des Moines and parked by a seaside marina with a view of bobbing sail boats, cabin cruisers and power boats moored side by side under a star speckled sky. A couple of seagulls squawked overhead. It was the perfect place to dream about a new life, about sailing away together to exotic islands in the south Pacific . . . maybe to the island of Samoa where Vili's ancestors were from. In Samoa, they could rent a turtle shaped, open air, thatched house resting on poles over a turquoise lagoon. From their 'fale', they would look out at the coconut plantations climbing up the island's sunny slopes to the volcanic ridges in the panoramic distance. They would shower together under outdoor faucets, climb to the top of a towering waterfall, build sand castles on the white sand beaches. Mary and Vili curled up under a blanket with their dreams and their arms to keep each other warm in the back of the minivan.

A security guard saw the minivan bump over a curb when it first pulled into the marina. Figuring it was a drunk driver, the guard rang the police who swung by the marina to investigate. They shone a flashlight through the back window of the parked van and spotlighted two bodies under a blanket. Mary crawled out from under the blanket and quickly slid into the driver's seat. She lied to the police about Vili's age and told them he was 18. When the officers questioned Vili, he admitted that he'd just turned 13. Mary appeared to be naked beneath her T-shirt and explained that she and the boy were just sleeping and that she'd had a fight with her husband. The officers suspected they might have an X-rated situation on their hands and phoned Vili's mother, Soona. Mary spoke to Soona and upgraded the X-rated scene to a G-rating. No charges were filed and Mary breathed a sigh of relief. It was a close call.

'We made love in nearly every room of her home while her husband, Steve, was away,' Vili told the *Globe*. If this was rape, it felt good. It felt so good, they did it in the car, in the house, on the rooftop at sunset. 'At night, we sometimes had sex on the deck – and even in a swing hanging from a tree in her front yard. I knew what we were doing was wrong. But neither of us wanted it to end.' Like Rose in the movie *Titanic*, Mary was trapped in a suffocating relationship. Like Rose, she posed naked while Vili sketched her. Like 'Jack', Vili was a talented artist devouring her with his eyes and etching her on paper and in his mind for all eternity. Their ship started to sink almost as soon as they boarded it. Mary found out she was pregnant and confided her situation to her father, ex-congressman John Schmitz. She told him everything. John was supportive but cautioned that in the eyes of the law, she'd committed statutory rape and may already be under investigation and in big legal trouble. After cautioning her, John asked her the only question that really mattered to her. 'Do you love him?' Mary's expression said it all. 'Very well, then,' said the ex-congressman, 'after you're married, we'll just take this to the governor and ask for a pardon.'

LIKE THE TITANIC

The trouble started after Steve's mistress left him. 'That's when he started digging up anything he could on my business', Mary remembers. 'That's when he found my journal, my notes and my love letters. Steve read a letter Mary wrote to Vili that said, 'Do you remember . . . when we first saw the promise in each other's eyes . . . when we discovered everything was the same . . . and each question we asked each other only strengthened the truth we knew . . . that feeling inside when one little touch and a look said it all . . . and how fragile our language became when we realized how deep our feelings were. Do you remember . . . when we knew we needed each other every day, constantly . . . when "I love you" was disguised so we could say it all day in front of everyone . . . and all the love songs seemed to have been written just for us . . . the only explanation was that we were together in another life.'

A love poem from Vili to Mary expressed the intense feelings of a boy who was mature beyond his years. He wrote, 'This love is more than just how our flesh looks or our age. All that matters is how we finish the puzzle, the missing pieces now completed . . . I hold your love within me forever and we're together always as one . . . My love for you will never be parted, through death, never. We love together in oceans . . . that is what makes the waves so loud . . . .'

The most incriminating letter was the one Mary wrote to Vili following her meeting with her father. It was a letter that could just as easily have been written by Bill Clinton to a woman almost thirty years his junior. 'Maybe I am already under investigation and don't know it yet. I need a plan and a life-and-death promise from you about this. You don't need to do anything except promise on your life not to ever, ever, no matter how someone questions you, to ever tell about us – not even a kiss can be told.' Steve went berserk. It was like the moment Mr Robinson found out that the neighbour boy, Dustin Hoffman, had been bonking Mrs Robinson and his daughter in *The Graduate*. Steve got in his car and burned rubber over to Vili's house. According to the police report, Steve 'knocked on the door and asked him to come outside saying he wanted to talk to him. Steve then asked Vili if he and Mary were having an affair'. Vili looked up and saw the fury on the towering ex-football player's face. 'He told me "I know you're sleeping with my wife, so don't lie to me". I was scared, remembering what

Mary said about her going to jail if anyone found out she was having sex with a guy my age. My mind was racing all over the place. I didn't know what Steve was capable of doing. Mary had told me about their heated arguments, so I kept my distance.' In Mary's version of the confrontation, her husband said to Vili, 'She's mine forever,' and Vili shot back, 'Not a chance, buddy'. Steve was unaware at the time that his wife was already six months pregnant with the boy's baby. One of Steve's interfering relatives cried 'rape' and filed a complaint with the Washington State Department of Child Protective Services. The complaint triggered a police investigation and Vili was hauled out of middle school. Investigators grilled the boy for three hours until they squeezed a confession. 'Yes', he had sex with Mrs Letourneau. 'Yes', Mrs Letourneau was carrying his baby. The police phoned Vili's mother who told them Mary Letourneau needed help.

THE ICEBERG

On 26 February, 1997, Mary's life spun out of control. She was interrupted at a faculty meeting and instructed to go the principal's office. Her immaculate reputation as a hard-working, devoted teacher came under fire. A detective asked Mary point blank if she'd had sexual relations with Vili Fualaau, a 13-year-old student at Shorewood. Mary felt a sinking feeling in the pit of her stomach. Her ship had hit an iceberg.

Mary was arrested and placed under a court order not to reside in the same house with minors, including her own children. She was ordered to avoid all contact with Vili Fualaau and his family. Mary immediately violated the court order and phoned Soona. She pleaded for a chance to explain. Two days after her arrest, she and Soona met in a restaurant. Soona was unforgiving. She felt betrayed and wanted to 'strangle' Mary for violating her son.

Mary told her that she and Vili were soulmates, that they were in love with each other. Was that so hard to understand?

Mary slept in her parked car outside her house in Normandy Park so she could take care of her children without violating the court order. She hired a lawyer, David Gerkhe, but first wanted to know if he considered her a 'pervert'. Gerkhe replied no, that in a lot of cultures and in a different era, her relationship with the boy would be perfectly normal, legal and encouraged'.

THE 'N' WORD

Steve perceived the sexually precocious Samoan-American boy a rival. During one of his frequent rages, he asked Mary if the 13 year old boy was bigger (better endowed) than him. On 9 May, police got a report about a domestic dispute at the Letourneau house. Mary was eight months pregnant at the time and Steve was calling her baby the 'n' word in front of the kids. He drove his fist into her stomach and shouted, 'We want to see the law bury you, and it can't happen too soon.' By the time the police arrived, Steve had already raced off in his car. 'He wanted me to miscarry,' said Mary. 'He knew I was prone to it, and he'd get rough with me, hoping I'd miscarry the baby.' The investigating officer observed a large red mark on Mary's stomach and asked her if she wanted to press charges. Mary declined. Later that night, Steve pulled up in front of the house in his car. He was drunk and began quarrelling with Mary again. As the argument escalated, Steve stepped on the gas and knocked his wife to the ground as he sped away. A neighbour rescued Mary and rushed her to the hospital, fearing she'd lose her baby.

In May, 1997, shortly before Vili's fourteenth birthday, Mary gave birth to a healthy baby girl and called her Audrey

Lokelani. When Soona picked up her grandchild and held her in her arms, her attitude towards Mary changed. 'Seeing that beautiful little girl softened any hard feelings toward Mary . . . I guess I'm a romantic at heart . . . if someone truly loves someone, age doesn't matter. My son's romance with his teacher was based on true love, not lust.'

FROM CLASSROOM TO COURTROOM

A crisis intervention team was on call when classes at Shorewood Elementary School resumed that fall. Vili wasn't prepared for the cruel jokes and whispers that followed him into the classroom, along school corridors and out into the street. He was suspended for missing classes and later arrested on a minor second-degree robbery charge. A Child Protective Services report cited his mother for beating him. Arrangements were made for Vili to study under a private home tutor.

In August, 1997, Mary Kay Letourneau pleaded guilty to two counts of child rape. Vili saw the face of the woman he loved on television, the face of the woman he was told he would never see again. She was right there in front of him as big as life on the news hour dressed in an orange V-neck prison uniform. Her head was hung and she looked heartbroken. Vili listened to her tearful, trembling voice as she told King County Superior Court judge, Linda Lau, 'I did something that I had no right to do. Morally or legally, it was wrong. I give you my word that it will not happen again. Please help me.' Mary added remorsefully, 'I think what I've done was horrible . . . and I wouldn't want anyone to think I believe it's acceptable. It's not.' Soona was present in the courtroom. She told the court, 'I think Mary has been punished enough for her mistake . . . Mary's not a bad person, she's just a human being that made a terrible mistake.'

Judge Linda Lau gave Mary the benefit of the doubt. She conditionally suspended all but six months of a seven-and-a-half-year sentence. One of the conditions of her release was that she take a drug medication, Depakot, to treat a bipolar disorder. Mary had been diagnosed with the disorder (a form of manic-depression) known to cause dramatic mood swings and reckless, hypersexual behaviour. A second condition of her release stipulated that she have no further contact with Vili Fualaau or with minors.

Audrey was placed in Soona's custody. Vili helped his mother and older sister feed and diaper her. He was an adoring father. His own father, Luaiva, hadn't been so adoring. After settling in Hawaii, Luaiva abandoned Soona and the kids and spent his life in and out of prison for crimes ranging from robbery and assault to beating up a former girlfriend to battery and false imprisonment. Soona moved to Seattle and raised her four children as a single parent through part time jobs, welfare, food stamps and help from the Samoan-American community. She officially divorced Vili's father in 1996. Luaiva is currently serving time in a Texas prison. He claims to have fathered 18 children by six different women.

REGISTERED SEX OFFENDER

Mary protested when the Special Sex Offender Sentencing Alternative required her to tell her kids that she was a rapist. 'Since when do people who love each other have to defend it?' King County prosecutor, Lisa Johnson, who handled Mary's case said, 'she (Letourneau) doesn't believe she needs treatment because she doesn't believe she did anything wrong.' Sexual abuse expert, Florence Wolfe, was not surprised by Mary's attitude. Women sex offenders often enter treatment convinced they had a love affair and 'it often takes them a long time to realize it was exploitation.' Seeing the victim as unusually mature and the relationship as an affair is a typical 'cognitive distortion'. Lucy Berliner, Research Director of the Harbourview Center for Sexual Assault, pointed out that 'exploiting a young teenager's desire to be older, to be liked, to be accepted is the currency of the sex offenders who prey on children of that age.'

Mary was a reluctant participant in the sex offender programme. She was expected to participate in groups and to be brutally honest and confrontational with others in her group. In many ways, Mary wasn't like the others in her group. She didn't fit the general profile of a sex offender. Sex offenders are typically predators who are active in their late teens and strike victim after victim. Mary Letourneau had no previous record of child sexual abuse.

After serving only two and a half months of a seven-and-a-half-year prison sentence, Mary completed the sex offender program and went to live with a former teaching colleague, Beth Adair, in a cottage-style home in south Seattle. Beth had stuck by Mary and defended her when other teachers had turned against her. She was a true friend who visited Mary in prison with Soona and the baby. Beth was certain that it was Steve's abuse that had caused Mary to reach out to Vili.

On 2 January, within days of her release, Mary discontinued her bipolar medication. The side effects were making her hair fall out. She rebelled against treatment counsellor, Terry Copeland, and insisted she didn't have a problem. At a friend's suggestion, Mary bought a pager and gave the number to Vili. 'He called me with some needs, and I came'. Three days after her thirty-sixth birthday, he told her he was in trouble and didn't want to go home. From the moment she was released, Mary arranged secret rendezvous with the boy. On the night of 2 February, they saw a movie, then drove to a grocery store to pick up some food and beer. Mary wanted to help him with his problems so he could 'get home to his family, home to his baby.' Time flew when they were together. It was after 2 a.m. and they were still sitting in the car talking. Few people listened to Vili's problems but Mary was special. She was his soulmate. She listened . . . and as she listened, she was violating Judge Lau's condition for her freedom.

A police car was cruising the streets of a south side Seattle neighbourhood searching for a stolen vehicle. The officers spotted a suspicious looking silver Volkswagen Fox parked on a quiet residential street in upscale Seward Park. The parking lights were aglow and the windows were steamed up. The police shone their flashlights inside and peered in. It was a déjà vu. Frozen in the beam of the flashlight was the familiar face of an attractive, infamous 36-year-old blond – Mary Kay Letourneau. The same Samoan-American boy, now 14, who she'd recently been convicted of raping was sitting beside her. Less than one month after her release from prison, the police caught Mary Letourneau red-handed violating the court order and possibly violating the boy again. They searched the vehicle and found $6,200 in cash inside a strongbox, a load of baby clothes and Mary's passport hidden under the floor mat. At first, Mary and Vili gave the officers false names and insisted they weren't having sex – just talking. By all appearances, it looked as though Mary and her juvenile lover were at it again, this time with plans of fleeing the country with their eight-month-old baby.

BEAUTY IS THE BEAST

On 6 February, Mary Letourneau was back on television dressed in orange V-neck jail house fashions and competing for airtime with the President of the United States. Bill Clinton was ducking accusations that he committed adultery by having sex with Monica Lewinsky, a young White House intern who was almost 30 years his junior. Even though Vili was twenty-two years Mary's junior, Mary didn't have the benefit of executive privilege. Judge Linda Lau called Mary's behaviour, 'egregious and profoundly disturbing' and sent her back to the Washington Corrections Center for Women in Gig Harbor to serve the remaining seven years and five months of her seven-and-a-half-year sentence for child rape. Lau made it painfully and abundantly clear that Mary would have no further contact with Vili. 'This case is not about a flawed system. It is about an opportunity you foolishly squandered,' scolded Lau.

The Letourneau story wasn't a 'Beauty And The Beast' story. It was a 'Beauty *Is* The Beast' story about a beautiful woman turned sexual predator and cradle robber. The story had a dash of incest, a touch of mental illness and a pinch of forbidden passion that catered to the perverse tastes of TV trash viewing audiences. It also raised legal and moral issues that sparked heated national debate. The media pounced on it like a pack of drooling pit bulls. Oprah, Dateline, Geraldo, and even the New York Times went on a feeding frenzy. They couldn't get enough of it and neither could the public.

Mary and Vili were approached about movie deals, book deals, story deals. *Spin* Magazine even offered to publish Vili's art work. A Seattle television station chased after him for an interview and publicized his comments when he innocently compared his relationship with Letourneau to 'Romeo and

Juliet'. Journalists joked about the comparison. 'Let's see. Juliet – a teacher, marries and gives birth to the daughter of Romeo who is a sixth grader. Okay – so it's not like Romeo and Juliet'. Others joked that Mary was assured a date for the school prom and that her pregnancy was part of a school science project. *Mirabella* Magazine identified a drink served by a Seattle restaurant called 'Mary Kay Letourneau Delight' – twelve year old Scotch on the rocks with a cherry.

A SECOND ICEBERG

With the fighting spirit of a Xena warrior princess, Mary took on the media, the justice system and the mental health profession and deflected the blows single handedly. She appeared on the Oprah Winfrey show and called the sex offender programme an 'oppression-valued obedience programme.' She announced that she would be appealing her conviction and declared that her 14-year old lover was 'the love of my life.' She told Oprah that she wanted to marry him and didn't think it was out of line because of his maturity level. When Oprah asked her if her love for the boy was worth imprisonment, Mary replied, 'It's worth it for the fact that I'm able to stay true to myself . . . ' Oprah then asked Mary if she'd had sexual contact with the boy in the car on the night in question. Dodging an answer that might prove incriminating, Mary replied, 'I think we should leave it at that.' The incriminating answer came several weeks later when it was discovered that Letourneau was pregnant for a second time. A sonogram revealed that she would be expecting another baby in November.

Not since 1980 when Mount St Helens erupted like an H-bomb had the northwest been jolted with such explosive news. Mary's second pregnancy with the underage boy grabbed global headlines and sent shock waves across America. Vili admitted that he'd had sex with Mary during the month that she was out on parole. Childless women, unable to conceive after years of marathon fornicating, were in awe of Mary like she was Isis, the goddess of fertility.

NOT A MALE 'LOLITA'

Vili Fualaau was nameless and faceless when the scandal first broke because of a law protecting the anonymity of minors. He appeared on television with his face concealed by computer generated distortions and pleaded to viewers in a deep, soft spoken voice, 'I want people to stop seeing me as a victim. My life is going to be fine. Mary didn't harm me in any way.'

Both fascinated and repelled by the illicit union, the public pressured the media for the uncensored details. Who was the mysterious underage boy? Did he look like Leonardo DiCaprio? Who came on to whom? Where did it happen? How did it happen? How many times did it happen? What was it like the first time? Mary's lawyer, David Gerkhe, was swamped with offers from Germany, Australia, TV Brazil and Radio Argentina, from magazine publishers and TV talk shows like Jerry Springer and Montel Williams. Everybody wanted a piece of it. They'd fly her there, put her up, come to her. Overwhelmed by the avalanche of offers, Gerkhe's law office hired a special media advisor to deal with the flood of requests.

Vili's family was struggling financially. They decided to see a lawyer and to authorize the sale of Vili's story and family photos to the *Globe* tabloid magazine. In exchange for revealing Vili's name, identity and story, the *Globe* agreed to set up a trust fund for Mary and Vili's baby daughter, Audrey. For the first time, Vili's name and face became public. He was unveiled in the glare of twinkling flashbulbs, clicking cameras and poking microphones. The media peered and pried, nudged and pushed until everything that had once been personal, private and sacred between Mary and Vili . . . their love letters, their treasured moments together, their entire lives . . . were auctioned off to the highest bidder. Unveiled at last, Vili was not the boy centerfold, the Calvin Klein underwear model or the male 'Lolita' that the public had imagined him to be. Instead, he was an average looking kid with a foreign looking face and a ponytail.

SUPERSTARDOM

Mary's lawyers seized an opportunity to change Mary's public image from the crazy, handcuffed, child rapist that viewers had observed on TV news shows into a caring, feeling, living, breathing, sensitive human being. Mary Letourneau had been an active, involved parent before her arrest who brought her four children to Disneyland in 1997. She escorted them to church on Sundays and imbued them with good Christian values. A friend recalled that 'on her refrigerator, she stuck a list of rules she wanted her children to follow . . . It listed things like not to raise their voices and to share and to do their chores.' Mary was a devoted mother who truly missed her kids.

As the public got to know Mary Letourneau, they began to see her as she saw herself – like Rose, the tragic figure in the movie blockbuster, *Titanic*. Like Rose, Mary was born into a life of privilege. Like Jack, Mary's young lover, Vili Fualaau, came from a poor, working-class family.

The controversial pair appeared together on the pages of entertainment magazines juxtaposed in glossy color photographs next to their movie star idols – Leonardo DiCaprio and Kate

Winslet. Their adoring faces decorated supermarket shelves and international newsstands. Mary and Vili were newsworthy. They would be remembered. They were immortalized together, forever. In spite of the law, the prison bars and judge Linda Lau's admonitions, the unlikely couple were inseparably together.

As much as the media used the controversial pair for its own ends, Mary and Vili also used the media for their own ends. The law could keep them apart but the media would keep them together. Reporters and the print media were their messengers. The television screen was their window through which they could see each other. Using secret signs, codes, gestures and word symbols, they could speak to each other in a language of personal messages that only they could understand.

Steve Letourneau decided to hitch a ride on the money trail and began writing a book about his joyless marriage. 'Our marriage was not complete bliss', admitted Steve. When the press asked him how he felt about his wife's second pregnancy with the same boy, Steve replied, 'I'm kind of speechless.' Steve's new female companion, Kelly Whalen, was equally as speechless but said, 'It's bad enough that they're having to deal with the first sibling – and now a second?' Mary's mother-in-law, Sharon Hume, was not so speechless. She had lots of mother-in-law things to say about her daughter-in-law. Sharon summed it up by saying, 'She's one sick person'.

Steve put the three bedroom house in Normandy Park up for sale, sued for divorce and moved to Anchorage, Alaska, with the four kids. He felt that the kids were 'handling it pretty well, considering their anger', although his eldest son, Steve Jr, 'can't comprehend what she's done.' Mary believed 'the children are hurting mainly from decisions [Steve] has made . . . I am doing everything I can to help them through this . . . He is doing everything he can . . . to project blame onto me.' Even though Mary is behind bars and has lost the freedom to choose when she sleep, eats and showers, she enjoys at least one consolation – 'I'm glad I'm freed from that selfish bastard'. Mary was unashamed of her second pregnancy and called it 'a gift from God.' When Vili heard the news, he felt like a fool. Mary had assured him she was using natural birth control. 'Now I'm surprised I have another daughter,' he told reporters. Michele Jarvis, Mary's best friend since childhood, commented that 'this baby she is carrying is the one thing that will keep her going . . . that if she didn't have this life inside of her, she would have cracked up.'

IN HER FATHER'S FOOTSTEPS

A glimpse at Mary's family history dispels some of the mystery surrounding the scandal. Her maiden name was Mary Katherine Schmitz. She had four brothers and two sisters and grew up a child of privilege in Corona del Mar, a posh suburb of Orange County backdropped by tall swaying palm trees and rolling hills. The Schmitz family lived in an architectural dream home landscaped with olive trees and hibiscus blossoms. Her best friend, Michele Jarvis, sometimes stayed for sleepovers. After everyone had gone to bed for the night, the girls would sneak into the kitchen, raid the fridge and take a dip in the outdoor swimming pool. That same swimming pool became a death trap for Mary's three-year-old brother, Phillip. Phillip drowned in Mary's presence and the experience left her emotionally scarred. Her relationship with Vili Fualaau and her inordinate number of pregnancies (seven not including miscarriages) may have been attempts to deal with the loss and the guilt over her younger brother's death.

Mary's father, John Schmitz, was a former Republican congressman in Orange County, California. She adored her father. He was charming, handsome, successful, and an ambitious moral crusader who taught philosophy at California's Santa Ana College before being elected to public office. He was also a rigid Catholic, well known for his outspoken attacks on threats to public decency. His right wing extremism got him in hot water with gays, Jews and blacks. Schmitz accused Martin Luther King of being a liar and called all homosexuals 'queers' and 'paedophiles'. He occasionally clicked his heels together, made straight arm-Hitler salutes and boasted about his proud German roots. The Jewish Defense League picketed his home and protested against his bigotry and anti-semitic comments. While the press waited on the front lawn for Schmitz to make a public statement of apology, young Mary was upstairs in the family's house defiantly cranking up the German marching music. In 1972, John Schmitz ran for President of the United States on the right wing American Independent Party ticket. John's moral and political positions became so extreme that he was eventually asked to leave the right wing John Birch Society.

Mary Kay's mother (also named Mary) was equally as stern as her father in raising the kids and ran a repressive Catholic household. She was also politically active and appeared on national television as an outspoken critic of the Equal Rights Amendment. Mary felt her mother didn't devote enough attention to her children's emotional needs. Both her parents travelled a lot and Mary was often left in the care of her three older brothers. She later revealed to a counsellor that she had an incestuous relationship with one of her older brothers at age seven. Gloria Allred, a feminist lawyer and former friend of the family, felt John and Mary's treatment of the kids was heavy handed. 'John and Mary were so ideologically strict, so repressive . . . I'm sure [Mary Kay] never felt comfortable talking to them about things she might have been feeling.' Her father made 'sex' a taboo subject at home and opposed sex education in the schools. He shuffled Mary between Catholic schools in an effort to preserve her innocence.

By all outward appearances, the Schmitz family hailed from the black and white town of Pleasantville. Mary's father nicknamed her 'Cake' and the name stuck like icing. In high school, Cake was a wholesome, preppy cheerleader – attractive, personable, charming, popular and very religious – just like her dad. Then, in 1982, her beloved father's true hypocritical stripes started showing. The media caught him with his pants down and exposed him for the sinner and the hypocrite that he was. John Schmitz had the gall to preach to America about public decency and, all the while, carry on a 'not so decent' extramarital affair. For nine long years, John cheated on his wife with an ex-student from his political science class. During their secret nine-year affair, he fathered not one but *two* children with his student who was later charged with child neglect. The public was outraged. The man who had fought so vigorously to ban sex education in the schools and had preached about moral responsibility and decency, had been practising the same sins he'd been denouncing. John's political halo quickly lost its shine. Like Jimmy Swaggart, he clasped his hands together, got down on his knees and begged the good Lord for forgiveness. Unforgiving voters were unimpressed and gave Presidential candidate and congressman Schmitz the boot after only one term in office.

BITTERSWEET
Mary remained loyal and deeply committed to her father throughout his tar and feathering in the early eighties. By all

intents and purposes, she seemed to have put the scandal behind her. 'I'm not excusing what Mary Kay did, and I'm not a psychiatrist, but I can understand how she could have crossed the line the same way her father did,' commented Gloria Allred. Double life? Adulterous sex? Teacher-student? Two pregnancies? Public scandal? Could the parallels be explained away as just a coincidence?

Mary objected when the media dredged up her father's past all over again in search of an explanation for her scandalous behaviour. 'He had a right to die with dignity,' she protested. Whether conscious or unconscious, Mary must have been harbouring some degree of deep-seated hostility over her father's deception and public humiliation. But the embarrassment and humiliation that her father heaped on his family was a drop in the bucket compared to Mary's scandal. If the motives for statutory rape are power and anger, Mary had good reason to be powerfully angry at the men in her life. Her sex scandal may have been, coincidentally, a bittersweet vehicle for getting even not just with her father but with her husband, Steve, who had flagrantly run around with other women during their marriage and had verbally and physically abused her in front of the children. The whole world now knew about Steve's abuse, his rages, his affairs and his masculine insecurities. The whole world now knew that his wife had fornicated in every room of their house with a 12-year old boy while he was at work and that the boy impregnated her – not once, but twice! Was there an ounce of revenge in the mix?

EQUAL UNDER THE LAW

The Letourneau case sparked lively national debate over whether Statutory Rape laws should apply equally to both genders. Statutory rape laws were originally designed to prevent unwanted teen pregnancies and to protect impressionable, young girls from coercive older men. Apart from power motives, men who commit statutory rape, generally do it for sex. Women do it for love, but in the eyes of the law, 'love' is not a mitigating circumstance.

The law takes only two factors into consideration in determining guilt or innocence – chronological age and sexual intercourse. Chronological age measures the age of the body from the time of birth, although a person's chronological age and mental age (emotional maturity level) may be very different. Mary Letourneau's mental age was compatible and perhaps even comparable to Vili's age. In most states, the age of consent is between 16 and 18. Any child under the age of consent is not considered mature enough to consent to sexual intercourse, yet in many other cultures of the world, the sanctioned readiness for sexual intercourse is determined by the sexual maturity of the human body. Some girls start to menstruate and some boys start to ejaculate as early as ten years of age. In Samoa, the homeland of Vili's ancestors, sex was encouraged in adolescenthood despite the puritanical ideologies taught to them by Christian missionaries. Many couples in turn-of-the-century North America married and procreated at age 16 and younger. In 1917, Mary Onesi became the 13 year old bride of Paul Onesi. The Onesis settled in Niagara Falls and are now the longest married couple in North America after 80 years of marriage.

PAST LIFE

Mary believes 'there is no age in pure, true love.' Her relationship with Vili, she said, transcended societal boundaries and even time itself. Vili told the press that he and Mary were soul spirits who already had 'about ten children' together. 'I knew we were together before this life.' Soona claims that her son is an old soul in a young body – older, wiser and more mature than Mary's ex-husband, perhaps. His friends even nicknamed him 'Buddha'.

If Vili is an old soul incarnated in a young man's body, Mary may be a young soul incarnated in an older woman's body. Her youthful exuberance, vitality, gushing love letters, back-seat car sex and risk-taking rebelliousness smack of teenage love, passion and Harlequin romance. At age 36, Mary experienced that swept-away 'falling in love' feeling for the first time in her self-sacrificing, people-pleasing, rule-abiding life.

STATUTORY RAPE – THE GENDER ISSUE

Comparing a 13-year-old girl's loss of virginity to an older man and a 13-year-old boy's loss of virginity to an older woman is like comparing root canal surgery to a victory celebration. Older women don't ejaculate, don't impregnate, don't break hymens and don't cause bleeding. Typically, the male virgin is sexually aroused, anxious to prove his manhood and experiences the pleasure of a sexual orgasm. By contrast, the 13-year-old female virgin experiences painful penetration, a ruptured hymen, bleeding and a possible pregnancy that could negatively impact her entire life. Her chances of experiencing a sexual orgasm are practically nil. The risk and damage to girls including self esteem and reputation damages far exceeds the risk and damage to boys.

The Letourneau case raises more than just the gender question. The most fundamental question in the Mary Letourneau case is whether her punishment for falling in love and having sexual intercourse with Vili Fualaau fits the crime and whether a crime was even committed. Was the boy harmed when Mary Letourneau submitted to his sexual advances or was he harmed by the court's decision to severely punish her for making love with him? 'They say I'm a victim, but I'm not . . . I'm more of a victim without her,' Vili declared. 'Mary didn't take my childhood. I gave it away.' Violent rapists, paedophiles, murderers and hardened criminals have received lighter sentences than Mary Letourneau who served a seven-and-half-year prison term for child rape. With incest, child abuse, child neglect, child prostitution and teen pregnancies at epidemic levels, Mary Letourneau may be the political scapegoat for a frustrated criminal justice system.

IS IT LOVE OR RAPE?

Dr Fred Berlin, founder of the Johns Hopkins University Sexual Disorders Clinic in Baltimore, was interviewed on the Sixty Minutes TV show about the Letourneau case. Berlin was asked if he considered Vili Fualaau a victim? 'Not every child is invariably or inevitably harmed by this kind of relationship,' answered Berlin who stressed that no adult should ever put a child at such risk. 'It was wrong but not necessarily permanently damaging.' In answer to the question, 'Is it rape or is it love?' Dr Berlin suggested 'it can be both. It doesn't mean that our only option when this situation develops is to get angry and to throw away the key. If indeed this is a troubled person, getting them help, trying to rehabilitate them, helping them to become a productive member of society is a very valid part of our system.' Dr Berlin didn't consider Mary a risk to other children in the community. 'The sense I get with this woman is that she really fell in love with this youngster . . . I don't think that it's a healthy thing for her to feel that way, but we can't always control who we fall in love with or how.'

Dan Satterberg of the King County prosecutor's office in Seattle warned that, 'The danger of this case is that it tends to undermine the seriousness of sex abuse cases involving adolescent boys.' But Mary Letourneau didn't fit the profile of other sex offenders. She had no previous record of sexually abusing children and no history of collecting, watching or masturbating to kiddie porn, of sexually fantasizing about children or of coercing or lusting after them. Less than five per cent of all known paedophiles are women. 'We treat this as just another cognitive disorder,' said treatment specialist, Roger Wold. 'What we're dealing with here is obviously not "love" as most people define it.'

'Is love an illness?' asks Mary. When her relationship with the 12-year-old boy first started, it felt natural to her. 'What didn't seem natural was a law forbidding such a natural thing.' The relationship developed as a relationship of 'mutual, consensual love.' The problem isn't the relationship. It's tradition, peer pressure and the law, says Mary. Susan Murphy, a Seattle school teacher who worked with Letourneau, believes that Mary truly is in love with the young man. 'You could not do the things that she has done. You could not give up what she gave up if you didn't believe that.' Comments from online visitors to the Mary Letourneau website ranged from 'horny slut' to 'you go girl!' Many rejected cosmic love, bipolar disorder and past lives as valid excuses. 'People say he [Vili] is mature for his age', said one online visitor. 'Well, that's bull! He wasn't even mature enough to use a condom!'

FORBIDDEN LOVE

Alexis Georgia was born in prison on 16 October 1998. Mary

was denied permission to breast-feed her second baby girl fathered by Vili. The baby was taken away from her and placed in the custody of the boy's mother, Soona. At the time of the birth, Vili was in Paris promoting a book that he and Mary co-wrote with the help of a ghost writer. French publisher Robert Laffont bought the book rights and reportedly paid a $250,000 advance. Mary was prohibited from receiving any profits from the sale of the book due to a Washington State law preventing criminals from profiting from their crimes. The book, called *Un Seul Crime, L'Amour* (Only One Crime, Love), was first published in French with a postcard insert for readers to petition for clemency. In the *Forbidden Love* English version of the book, Vili wrote, 'I was 12 years old and I had never fucked anyone. I wanted to see what it was like.'

After seven and a half years behind bars, Mary was released at 42 years of age. Vili promised he'd be waiting for her no matter how long it took. Just before dawn on the day of her release, Mary slipped unnoticed past the gawking hordes of looky-loos and reporters waiting patiently outside the Washington Corrections Center for Women. Vili, her then 21-year-old victim wasn't waiting for her. He was busy challenging a court order that barred Mary from contacting him. As a condition of her release, Letourneau was forbidden contact with her former pupil and father of two of her children. Vili's attorney, N. Scott Stewart, filed a motion to vacate the no-contact order. The motion argued that Vili Fualaau 'does not fear Mary K Letourneau' and added that the only basis for criminal charges was Vili Fualaau's age. 'He is now an adult and, as an adult, is requesting that the court allow him to be associated with other adults of his own choosing, specifically ' Mary K. Letourneau'.

LOVE, RAPE AND MARY LETOURNEAU

Letourneau, who sang in the choir and recorded books-on-tape for the blind while behind bars, 'wants to try to build a normal life,' said Seattle attorney Anne Bremner. A normal life would be next to impossible for Mary with the paparazzi on her doorstep and with authorities notifying her new neighbors that a registered sex offender had moved into their neighborhood.

On May 21 2005, Mary Kaye Letourneau married her former student who she was convicted of raping. It was a tightly guarded ceremony at the Columbia Winery about 20 miles north-east of Seattle. Letourneau's teenage daughter, Mary Claire, from her first marriage, was the official maid of honor and the couple's daughters, Audrey, 8, and Alexis Georgia, 7, were flower girls.

4

OUTSMARTED

Male culture has built an amazingly large mythology
around the idea of feminine evil . . . The things they fear,
they will find if they open Pandora's box.

Jean Baker Miller
American psychiatrist

A sexy female teacher deflowers a love-struck boy – but the
teacher is not Mary Letourneau. She's a different teacher in a
different town with a different motive – murder. Her name is
Pamela Smart and her love-triangle story of sex, lies and murder
became the subject of Joyce Maynard's novel, *To Die For*.
Maynard's novel blames a condition called 'media overload' for
erasing the boundaries that separate the real from the make-
believe. She writes about the confusion felt by the love-struck
boy's mother who says, 'One minute, you're sitting there
reading some article in a magazine about someone, the next
thing you know they're putting handcuffs on your son. It
doesn't feel like your real life, you know? It feels like you're on
a show, too. Only there's no commercials and it doesn't end.'

NO COMMERCIALS
It happened in the town of Derry in the final days of Desert
Storm. General Schwarzkopf had just finished giving Saddam

Hussein a good military spanking and New Hampshirites were switching channels from smart bombs on CNN to Pamela Smart on their local channels. The sexy, petite, not-so-smart, 23-year-old high school teacher was on trial for conspiring to murder her husband, Greggory Smart, with the help of her underage student lover. In the state of New Hampshire, the legal age of consent is sixteen, but statutory rape wasn't on the minds of prosecutors who were after something much bigger — a slam dunk murder conviction.

Pamela Wojas was daddy's little princess. She grew up in suburban Miami, Florida, the second of two children born to airline pilot, John Wojas, and his wife, Linda. 'She was the most loveable, friendly kid,' recalls John who worried about his daughter's safety because of Miami's soaring crime rate and big city violence. While Pamela was in eighth grade, the family relocated to the peaceful, scandal-free town of Windham, New Hampshire, where church bells ring on Sundays and where the four seasons feature fluttering crimson leaves in autumn, snow blanked rooftops in winter, springtime's maple sugar harvest and summer sunsets on tidal inlets.

Pamela enrolled at Derry's Pinkerton Academy where she excelled as an honor-role student and became a class officer. She was 'extremely energetic, very involved and always smiling', remembers Lara Chulak, adding that Pamela was also manipulative at times, but never really hurt anybody. Others from Pinkerton felt that Pamela was full of herself and would do just about anything to get attention. Despite the whispers, Pamela instinctively knew that she was destined for a life of fame and glamour. Glamour in high school meant dating the captain of the football team and joining the cheerleader squad . . . so that's what Pamela did. She and her chum, Lara Chulak, twirled batons, smiled and shouted 'rah-rah-rah's' like pretty little wind-up dolls at Pinkerton's sports events and rallies. But twirling batons, shaking pom-poms, doing cartwheels and making razzle dazzle on the sidelines for the home-team boys wasn't Pamela's idea of stardom.

Pamela experienced her first taste of fame at Florida State University in Talahassee where she was accepted into the media program and took over as the university's radio station disc jockey. She had a passion for heavy metal rock music and for David Lee Roth, who at the time was the lead singer in the heavy metal rock band, Van Halen. Pamela blasted the air waves with whining guitars and lyrics that preached of decadence and cruel love. Like Wolfman Jack, she was christened with an on-air celebrity name and became known to her radio listeners as the 'Maiden of Metal'. Of course, the DJ job was just a stepping stone to something much bigger – Barbara Walters' job.

BON JOVI LOOKALIKE

While visiting her family in New Hampshire at Christmas break, the Maiden of Metal met Gregg Smart at a yuletide party. She looked at him – a rock n' roller with Bon Jovi shoulder length hair. He looked at her – a sexy little DJ from Florida State. There was instant chemistry. Both of them loved rock music. Both of them loved to party. Both of them loved to copulate like hamsters. After Pamela returned to Florida State, they kept their budding romance alive with phone sex and letters. Gregg worshipped Pamela almost as much as Pamela worshipped herself and he wasn't going to risk losing her to some hormone-crazed college jock. Gregg followed Pamela back to Talahassee and became her steady boyfriend and bodyguard while she finished her third year at Florida State. In January, 1988, Gregg asked Pamela Wojas, the 'Maiden of Metal', to become Mrs Gregg Smart.

After Pamela's graduation ceremony, the couple moved back to New Hampshire. Gregg shed his long Bon Jovi hair, changed into a shirt, suit and tie and got a yuppie job with the Nashua New Hampshire Life Insurance firm where his father worked. Pamela settled into a teaching job at Winnacunnet high school as the media coordinator and later became an advisor for Winnacunnet's alcohol and drug awareness program. Gregg's mother, Judith Smart, had second thoughts about her future daughter-in-law. 'She used to say to me, "I'm going to be another Barbara Walters. I don't know how I'm going to do it."' Settling down and raising a family seemed to be the last thing on the mind of the future Mrs Gregg Smart. In May, 1989, Gregg and Pamela said 'I do' and bought a condo together. Pamela wanted a dog . . . not just any dog. Pamela wanted a glamorous, pure-bred dog. She bought a shih-tzu and named him, 'Halen', after the heavy metal rock band. Only seven months after the wedding, Gregg's parents noticed that the marriage was in trouble. Judith Smart confided to her husband, 'I hate to say this, but something's not right. They just got married, and already they're spending their week-ends apart.' Gregg was starting to look painfully ordinary to Pamela with his ordinary haircut and his ordinary job. They were living in an ordinary neighbourhood in an ordinary condo doing ordinary things. When Gregg confessed to having an 'ordinary affair' while he was out of town on a business trip, Pamela was out-raged. She told Gregg she wished she'd never married him. But divorce wasn't an option since divorce meant failure and Pamela never failed at anything she did. When push came to shove and she had to choose between divorce and murder, Pamela chose murder . . .

DEADLY LOVE TRIANGLE

The thirteen-day murder conspiracy trial became New Hampshire's biggest media event since the presidential primary. *Entertainment Tonight* set up a satellite dish in the parking lot of the drab Rockingham County Superior Court House in the historic town of Exeter. People were lining up at 2 a.m. for courthouse seats to watch the unfolding drama with its graphic testimonials of back-seat car sex and impromptu strip acts. In the shadow of the US heartland, passion, lies and murder captured national attention as TV and newspaper reporters swarmed Exeter's courthouse for the latest trial scoop. The *Boston Herald* even set up a 900 number at 95 cents a minute for readers to call in their verdicts. Nancy Gibbs wrote an article for *Time* magazine: 'New Hampshire – In the town of Derry. Pamela Smart, a 23-year-old high school instructor with big brown eyes, Gainsborough ringlets, and a taste for heavy metal music, deflowered a 15-year-old student'. Another reporter wrote, 'She used sex and lies to manipulate the boy as their relationship turned from innocent friendship to deadly romance'. TV viewers tuned in to the jam-packed courtroom and listened as the prosecution told a chilling tale of a marriage gone homicidally wrong. Pamela Smart was typecast by prosecutors as a 'programmed robot' and a 'cool calculating operator' who had excelled in school with almost perfect grades. Prosecutor, Paul Maggiotto, warned the jury that Pamela planned to use her manipulative intelligence to try to pull one over on them. He argued that her motive for murder, once she got 'her hooks into Flynn's hormones', was to keep her affair with the love struck underage boy a secret even if it meant doing away with her husband. Divorcing Greggory Smart would have exposed her and ruined her good reputation in the Peyton Place community.

Gregg's parents, Judith and Bill Smart, sat in the courtroom and watched as their daughter-in-law stepped up onto the witness stand. She was smartly dressed, well manicured and wore a shiny gold crucifix around her neck as she raised her hand and swore on the Bible to tell the whole truth and nothing but the truth. Somehow they doubted it. Pamela Smart testified that she first became enamoured with her student, Billy Flynn, in the fall of 1989 while helping him and some other students prepare a video project for a Florida orange juice video contest. When Billy Flynn wasn't working on the video with Pamela, he was either out riding dirt bikes with his buddies, playing guitar, or listening to his favourite rock group, Mötley Crüe. Pamela's attraction to the fifteen year old boy intensified when she discovered their mutual interest in the same heavy metal rock bands – Van Halen, Mötley Crüe, Led Zeppelin and Bon Jovi. 'At the beginning we were just friends but things changed . . . he came along and made me feel special and made me feel a lot of things that I hadn't been feeling.' She claimed that although she was having an affair with Billy, she never stopped loving her husband and denied knowing anything about a plot to murder him. 'Gregg was really the first love in my life and I did give him my whole heart.'

DEFLOWERED

Even with his thin moustache and shag haircut, Billy Flynn looked a lot younger than his age. His small frame, sea-blue eyes and innocent schoolboy face made him look thirteen, not fifteen. Like most teenage boys, Billy Flynn had an indelible memory of his first sexual experience. Unlike most boys, Flynn was forced to recount that first sexual experience to a packed courtroom of strangers and to millions of television viewers huddled around their TV sets across America. Sitting tensely in the witness box, Flynn told the jury that as a sophomore at Winnacunnet high school in Hampton, he talked to media director, Pamela Smart, about participating in the production of an orange juice commercial for a school video project. They started spending a lot of time working on the video together and Flynn would sometimes visit Pamela at her condo during the week. On one occasion, Pamela invited him to her office and showed him some photographs of herself posing in a bra and panties. The photographs were originally intended as a gift for Gregg but since Gregg neglected to show his appreciation for them, Pam found somebody who would. She told Flynn to choose the one he liked best as she hummed 'Hot For Teacher' by Van Halen – 'Teacher needs to see me after school, I think of all the education that I missed, but then my homework was never quite like this'.

Pamela was like a Viagra overdose. She'd wear tight sweaters, leather miniskirts and stone-washed jeans that looked like they'd been painted on. Flynn had a permanent 'boner' that just wouldn't go away. Things started to heat up the day Pamela gave Bill the keys to her Honda CRX. They drove to his house and went into Bill's room to work on the orange juice commercial. Alone in his room, Mrs Smart kissed her student for the first time.

In February of 1990, Pamela's husband, Gregg, went out of town to attend insurance classes in Rhode Island. Pamela invited Billy Flynn and Cecelia Pierce to spend the night at her condo. Cecelia, a plain looking 16-year-old eleventh grader, was Pamela's student aid, friend and confidante. Pamela confided to Cecelia about her plan to seduce Billy Flynn that night. The threesome shared a bottle of Southern Comfort, rented a steamy video called 9 $^1/_2$ *Weeks* starring Kim Basinger and Mickey Rourke and popped it into the VCR.

Flynn testified that after watching the movie, his teacher led him upstairs to her bedroom. She said she wanted to re-enact certain scenes from the movie as she turned on the stereo and started dancing seductively to Van Halen's 'Black and Blue'. Billy's chin hit the floor as he watched his teacher gyrating and swaying, writhing and undulating just like Kim Basinger in the movie. Mrs Smart tossed her blue negligee aside, then her undergarments. The boy's eyes feasted on her nakedness. His ears rang with the Van Halen lyrics – 'Slip n' slide, push it in, bitch sure got rhythm'. The message was loud and clear. His teacher wanted to ball him – 'Hooked into her system, don't draw the line'. His teacher wanted to ball him to the thump of Van Halen's 'Black and Blue' – 'The harder the better, let's do it 'till we're black and blue.'

'I was kind of shocked', testified Flynn. 'It's not everyday that a 15-year-old kid gets this twenty-two year old woman who is very attractive to say that she likes him.' Pamela got Billy to slowly rub an ice cube over her naked body just like Mickey Rourke had done to Kim Basinger. Prosecutor, Paul Maggiotto, asked Flynn what happened next. 'We had sex', replied Bill. 'Had you ever made love to another woman before?', asked Maggiotto. 'No, I hadn't,' replied Billy. Maggiotto then asked him if it was his first time and Billy answered, 'Yes, it was.'

Joyce Maynard describes the boy's deflowering in her novel based-on this case. 'My dick's so hard I feel like it could drill

80

through concrete', writes Maynard. 'All I wanted was to get inside her. I don't have time to look at her tits. She's so warm and tight all around me. It's like I'm in this underground tunnel and there's diamonds sparkling all around, and, I don't know, waterfalls, stars. I'm pumping her , and she's digging her fingers into my back . . . I can't hold back. Man, I just explode all over the place, like someone pulled the pin on a goddamn grenade.' Cecelia Pierce testified that she walked into Mrs Smart's bedroom and caught Pam and Billy in the act. 'I went upstairs and saw Bill and Pamela having sex . . . They had been up there for hours. They were naked on the floor. Pam was on top. She was bopping Bill'.

After hearing the steamy testimony, trial watchers rushed out and rented the movie *9 $1/_2$ Weeks*. It became the hottest movie rental in video stores in the entire state of New Hampshire. Everyone wanted to see the ice cube scene and watch Kim Basinger do her well-publicized striptease. The next day, people started lining up even earlier for a seat in the Rockingham courthouse. Judge Douglas Gray felt public interest in the proceedings and the excessive media invasion was becoming disruptive. 'We cannot hear the record because of the constant clicking of the shutters,' he told reporters angrily. 'I don't know how many pictures you need of one individual.' Interest in the proceedings grew as Flynn's testimony continued to thrill trial watchers with his descriptions of back-seat car sex. He confessed that he did it with his former teacher in the back seat of her Honda CRX about 'four to seven' times in a single afternoon. Flynn told the court that Pamela brought up the topic of offing Gregg soon after they started having sex. 'She actually asked you to kill Gregg?' asked Maggiotto. 'Yeah,' replied Flynn. 'She said the only way we can be together is if I kill Gregg.' She said that Gregg was physically and verbally abusive with her and that she was afraid to divorce him because she might lose the condo and the furniture and her shih-tzu, 'Halen'.

JUST ACT NORMAL

Pamela's 16-year-old student aide, friend and confidante, Cecelia Pierce, backed up Flynn's testimony. As a key witness for the prosecution, Pierce told the jury that Pamela confessed to her that she'd fallen in love with Flynn. She said her marriage was on the rocks but divorce wasn't a solution because of Gregg's possessiveness. He would never let her go and start a new life. Pierce told the court that she heard Pam and Bill plotting to kill Gregg but didn't take them seriously at first. Then, she heard Pamela tell Bill 'not to kill Gregg in front of the dog because it might traumatize the dog'. She made Bill promise to lock Halen in the cellar. Pierce realized Pamela wasn't kidding about the murder when she said to her, 'Oh, Bill's gonna go and kill Gregg tonight, but he can't get the car.'

Billy needed help. Murdering Pamela's husband was no easy proposition. He'd need a weapon, someone to drive the getaway car and someone to help him with the killing in case there were any unforeseen screw-ups. Billy rounded up a couple of friends that he knew he could trust – Vance Lattime, 18, and Patrick Randall, 17. Pamela told Cecelia that 'they were looking for a silencer and she said she had told the boys to make it look like a burglary'. She was dead against using a knife as a murder weapon because she didn't want Gregg's blood splattering on the furniture. According to Pierce, Pamela talked about the murder plans almost everyday.

In exchange for killing her husband, Pamela offered the boys $500 each and money from Gregg's life insurance policy. Car theft and vandalism were more in line with the boys' area of expertise but they decided they were up for the challenge. Patrick 'Pete' Randall told the court that Pamela masterminded every detail of the murder. He confirmed to the court that she instructed them to shoot Gregg instead of stabbing him so they wouldn't get blood on the sofa. Her instructions, testified Randall, were that 'we can go in . . . make sure we didn't turn on any lights . . . not to hurt her dog and that we could ransack the condo, take what we wanted and we could wait for Gregg to come home and when Gregg came home, we were to kill him'.

Before the murder, Pamela drove around with the boys so they could go over some last-minute details. She'd made a list. She was checking it twice and everybody knew she was naughty, not nice. She told the boys that she'd be at a school board meeting at the time of the killing so she would have an alibi. She asked them their opinion about how she should react when she came home from the school board meeting and discovered Gregg's dead body. 'She kept asking us how she should act,' said Lattime. 'She didn't know whether to scream, run from house to house or call the police. We told her just to act normal.' Pamela didn't know what they meant.

THE MURDER

On their first attempt, the boys lost their nerve and turned back. Pamela was furious. She screamed at Bill, 'You don't love me!' and threatened to end their relationship. Billy apologized and promised to get it right next time.

Gregg was busy planning a big wedding anniversary party to celebrate his first year of marriage. He planned to take Pam on a Florida vacation as an anniversary present. At nightfall on 1 May 1990, only a couple of days before the anniversary party,

Vance Latimme drove down a cul de sac and pulled into a shopping center plaza near the Summerhill condominiums. He dropped Billy Flynn and Patrick Randall off and waited in the getaway car as the boys changed into dark clothes near a row of dumpsters. They'd thought of everything. Even their fingertips were carefully wrapped in scotch tape beneath latex gloves to insure they wouldn't leave prints anywhere. Flynn scanned the area. The coast was clear. With hearts pounding and adrenalin pumping, the teenage killers crossed a field and entered the Smart condo through a back door that had been left unlocked. Pamela's neurotic little shih-tzu greeted them with flying leaps like he was trying to fetch their balls. They kicked him aside, ransacked the place, collected the loot and jewellery into a sack, then waited in the dark by the front door for Gregg to get home.

Gregg was visiting his parents and didn't get home until 9 p.m. Flynn and Randall heard Gregg's key in the lock and braced themselves. 'I heard Gregg walking towards the door,' testified Flynn, 'and uh, I heard the keys jingling outside the door and he opened the door.' The second Gregg got inside, the two boys pounced on him. Gregg struggled with them but Randall clutched onto a clump of his hair, slammed him against the wall and forced him to his knees. With a knife pressed to Gregg's throat, Randall ordered him to hand over the ring he was wearing. 'At first I thought it was just a normal gold ring but it turned out to be a wedding band,' testified Randall. 'And what happened at that time?' asked prosecutor Paul Maggiotto. 'He told me he wouldn't give it to me.' Maggiotto asked, 'Why not?' Randall replied, 'He said his wife would kill him.'

Contrary to Pamela's instructions, Randall had decided to slit Gregg's throat with a knife but chickened out at the last minute. Flynn reached inside his pocket for a concealed .38

calibre Charter Arms revolver that the boys had taken from Vance Lattime's father's gun collection. It was loaded with hollow point bullets known to be especially deadly. Flynn told the jury, 'I took the gun out of my pocket and I cocked the hammer back and pointed the gun at his head.' Gregg Smart was on his knees with the gun pointed at the back of his head, begging for his life. Maggiotto asked, 'After you pointed the gun at his head, what did you do?' Flynn tried to choke back the tears. 'I just stood there,' he answered with tears streaming down his face. 'How long?' asked Maggiotto. 'A hundred years it seemed like.' Flynn said he steadied the wavering gun, then hesitated and held back for a moment. The courtroom was pin-drop quiet as Flynn told the court in a quivering voice, 'I said, God forgive me.' When the prosecutor asked Flynn what happened next, Flynn sniffled and paused seven seconds before replying, 'I pulled the trigger.' Maggiotto asked him, 'Why did you say, "God forgive me"?' Flynn broke down and bawled like a baby. 'I didn't want to kill Gregg. I wanted to be with Pam and that's what I had to do to be with Pam but I didn't want to kill Gregg.'

Right after Flynn pulled the trigger on a kneeling, pleading Greggory Smart and fired a bullet, point blank, into his head, Gregg Smart slumped to the floor in the foyer. The two boys grabbed the bag of stolen items and high tailed it out the back door. They raced across the dimly lit back field spilling jewellery as they ran. They met up with 'J.R.' [Vance Latimme] waiting in the getaway car, piled in and sped away.

GRIEVING WIDOW

Pamela Smart, who had been attending a school board meeting, arrived at the condo about an hour and a half after Gregg's murder. She opened the door and saw her dead husband's body laying in the foyer in a pool of blood. As rehearsed, she ran from unit to unit in the condominium complex scaring the daylights out of her neighbours with her blood chilling shrieks. A neighbour called 911.

The police rushed to the scene of the crime and found Gregg Smart's body face down in the condo foyer with a bullet in his head. The back door was open and there was an empty jewellery box in the bedroom and clothes strewn everywhere. A butcher knife and other objects were retrieved as the police combed the area. Pamela called her mother and said, 'Mom, come quick. Gregg's dead!' She told the police that the condo had been burglarized and that her compact discs and $300 in jewellery were missing. Police investigators examining the crime scene, scratched their heads and asked themselves, 'what's wrong with this picture?'

Pamela's story was flawed right from the get-go. The police couldn't figure out why burglars would burglarize a condo with an entrance way in plain view of other townhouses in the complex. Why would they pack a firearm? And thirdly, why would they strike at night when residents were most likely to be home? Pamela insisted her theory was correct. 'I'm absolutely convinced that someone was burglarizing our home and Gregg just walked in,' she told the *Derry News*. Frustrated with the police investigation, Pamela continued to supply the media with her own spin on things.

On the day of Gregg's funeral, Pam led Gregg's parents, Judith and Bill Smart, to her husband's graveside and left a bouquet of red roses on their dead son's casket. Like the Queen at Princess Diana's funeral, Pamela was royally solemn and dignified. Gregg's father, Bill Smart, remembers feeling chills when he touched her. Something was frightfully wrong.

A couple of weeks after Gregg's murder, an anonymous female caller phoned the police with a tip. The voice said, 'There was a young man killed a couple of weeks ago . . . in his home . . . from what I have heard . . . the wife had planned this.' Pamela's grieving widow performance was cut short. Thirty miles away at Winnacunnet High School, an 18-year-old youth, Ralph Welch, overheard his buddies having the usual 'F . . . this and F . . . that' conversation. The subject turned to murder. Welch heard his friends say they murdered Gregg Smart. He heard them say that Flynn, Randall and Lattime had driven out to Pamela and Gregg Smart's condo and that one of them held Gregg down, one shot him and the other drove the getaway car.

After wrestling with his conscience, Ralph Welch blew the whistle on his buddies and turned them in like used beer cans. He told Vance Lattime's father that one of the guns from his collection was the murder weapon in the Greggory Smart murder. 'I couldn't believe my best friends had actually killed someone,' said Welch. On 10 June, 1990, Lattime's father turned the murder weapon over to police. The following day, ballistics experts matched the bullet that killed Greggory Smart with Lattime's revolver and the three boys were arrested. Pamela was shocked when she heard about the arrests. She needed to keep her affair with Billy under wraps.

THE SECRET TAPES

It didn't take Gil Grissom from *CSI* to figure out Pamela Smart's connection to Billy Flynn. Investigators already suspected Pamela had orchestrated her husband's murder and were hot on her trail – but they needed hard evidence. The murder trail led them to Pamela's 16-year-old student aide, Cecilia Pierce. During the police interview, Pierce admitted she knew about the murder but hesitated to squeal on Pamela because she thought of her as a friend. Pierce was plagued with doubts about the Winnacunnet teacher and the sincerity of their friendship. 'It was really bothering me that Pam had her husband killed,' she said and, 'her lover was in jail and she didn't care . . . and how was I supposed to believe that she was actually my friend?' Police asked Pierce to wear a wire and meet with Pamela to get the hard evidence they needed.

On 13 July 1990, the police outfitted Cecelia Pierce with a hidden microphone. Wearing the concealed wire, she met with Pamela and started a casual conversation with her. At an oppotune moment, she asked Pam what she expected her to say to the police if they ever questioned her. Pam replied abrasively, 'You're better off lying.' Wire tappers listened as Pam uttered the incriminating statements that sealed her fate. 'I hate the fact that you're probably gonna have to take a lie detector test but I don't know what to tell you . . . if you tell the fucking truth, you are probably going to be arrested,' warned Pam. 'You're gonna have to go and you're gonna have to send Bill, you're gonna have to send Pete [Randall], you're gonna have to send J.R. [Latimme] and you're gonna have to send me to the fucking slammer for the rest of our entire life.'

According to Pierce, she and Pamela had made an agreement that if Pierce were ever wired, she would signal to her. 'I'm afraid one day you're gonna come in here and you're gonna be wired by the fucking police and I'm gonna be busted . . . give me some signal that if you ever come down to me and you're wired that you're gonna give me,' demanded Pamela. 'I'll just wink', said Pierce reassuringly. 'For a few minutes, I had to think to myself, "Should I wink?" But I didn't wink.' Pierce then raised the possibility that Lattime might confess to the police. Pamela was getting agitated. 'That's when I'm going to be in trouble. That's when I'm going to be arrested, but I can probably get out of it because they are not going to have any proof, ya know.' Pamela comforted herself that her 'professional reputation' and the courses she taught would be enough reason for the cops not to take Lattime's word over hers. 'They are going to believe me,' she said smugly.

Pamela had thought of everything. Everything except the possibility that Cecelia, her friend and confidante, would squeal on her and send her to the slammer for the rest of her natural life. Police had what they needed – a taped statement showing Pamela had advance knowledge of the murder and a taped statement inducing a witness to lie. Pierce had extracted the slam-dunk confession that they needed. With the incriminating tapes in hand, the police arrested Pamela three months after Flynn's arrest and charged her with being an accomplice to first degree murder, conspiracy to first degree murder and witness tampering. According to Pam, they said, 'We have some good news and we have some bad news and they said the good news is that we solved the murder of your husband. The bad news is you're under arrest.' Pamela was frisked, handcuffed and never saw freedom again.

Patrick Randall confessed to the police that he held Greggory Smart down while Flynn pulled the trigger. William Flynn admitted he pulled the trigger. Vance Lattime Jr admitted he drove the getaway car. All three agreed to testify for the prosecution and pleaded guilty to lesser counts of second-degree murder. Flynn and Randall would serve at least 28 years and Lattime would serve a minimum of 18 years in exchange for telling the world the mathematics of their teacher's murder course.

THE PROSECUTIONS CASE

The prosecution argued that Flynn was willing to die for the woman he loved – or at least kill for her. They called Smart a female Svengali who purposely set out to capture the boy's heart and hormones by using her sexual prowess and position of power to dominate him sexually and psychologically. Once she got him hooked, she threatened to deprive him of a sexual fix unless he cooperated with her murder plan. Prosecutors charged that Smart masterminded the crime so that she could continue her love affair with Flynn and cash in on her husband's life insurance policy. With Gregg out of the way, she could keep her home, her furniture, her dog and her good reputation and for encores, she could play the poor suffering spouse. 'Deception is something she's very good at,' said Prosecutor Maggiotto of Smart who admitted hiding her sexual affair with Flynn even after he was arrested.

Pamela appeared unruffled on the stand as she described finding Gregg's body at the murder scene. Her steel expression and stone faced demeanour served to confirm the prosecution's depiction of her as a killer without a conscience who used an emotionally fragile teenage boy in her murder-for-hire scheme. Prosecutors asked Smart why she passed up opportunities to inform authorities of her affair with Flynn once he became implicated in the murder. She replied under oath, 'I was ashamed of the affair . . . I still am.' But, she said, 'I'm not the first person in America to ever have an affair.' Smart testified that although she had an affair with her husband's killer, she never stopped loving her spouse and denied knowing of the plot to murder him. Pam claimed to have patched things up with Gregg before the murder. She suggested that Flynn's motive for killing Gregg was to eliminate her husband as a romantic rival because Flynn felt that if he couldn't have her, nobody could.

A CASE FOR THE DEFENSE

Smart's attorney, Mark Sisti, called the prosecution's case 'the most vile concoction ever assembled in a courtroom in New Hampshire.' He characterized Flynn and his cohorts as 'cold blooded' teen hit men and 'thrill killers' who invented their twisted tale to escape first-degree murder convictions. A second lawyer for the defense, Paul Twomey, told the jurors that the teenage boys came in here and 'lied to you'. They framed Greggory's widow to avoid prison terms, plain and simple. Referring to the autopsy report, Twomey introduced an un-expected twist to the story. 'They did something else,' he said. 'They tortured that man some other way.' Twomey's statement raised speculation that the teenage killers may have tortured Gregg Smart. With a timely shriek, Gregg's mother, Judith Smart, cried out in court. Maggiotto jumped to his feet and objected to Twomey's statement. The prosecution's objection was sustained and the autopsy evidence suggesting that the boys tortured Gregg Smart was not admitted into evidence.

With the cool poise, eloquence and charm of her media idol, Barbara Walters, Pamela Smart sat in the witness box pleading her case and arguing her innocence. She was in the spotlight. She was center stage. The TV cameras were pointing at her. Millions of people were watching and listening and hanging onto her every word. The name 'Pamela Smart' was a household word and she was famous just as she'd predicted. But it was fame without glamour as Pamela spoke of the night she showed her 15-year-old student, Billy Flynn, the steamy video cassette of *9 1/2 Weeks* and the night she stripped naked for him in her blue negligee and banged him to the thump of Van Halen's Black and Blue.

Pamela denied the prosecution's assertions that she used sex and money to lure the boys into committing an execution style murder. 'If I was guilty, I would have pleaded guilty and plea bargained with the rest of them,' she said. 'I have no criminal record at all. I've never done anything in my life to indicate that I would just go from being a completely normal person to hiring people to kill somebody because I didn't feel like getting divorced. It just doesn't even make any sense.'

Under cross examination, Pamela defended herself against her secretly taped conversations with Cecelia Pierce. She said her admission that she knew about the murder was her own 'fabrication', a game aimed at finding out the truth about the case. She said she intentionally made those statements because she thought Pierce was involved in the murder and she wanted to find out what she knew. She claimed she was conducting her own investigation since the police kept her in the dark about the case. Like O.J. Simpson, Pamela was desperate to find the dirty dog who murdered her spouse in cold blood.

The jury listened as the prosecution played the secretly taped conversations between Pamela and Cecelia showing that Pamela had advance knowledge of the murder and tried to induce a witness to lie. With Pamela's undeleted expletives – she sounded more like Linda Blair from *The Exorcist* than a broken-hearted young widow. As Pamela Smart sat next to her defense attorneys looking metallically cool, Prosecutor, Diana Nicolosi, stood before the jury and pointed at her. 'It was that woman who initiated, orchestrated and directed the murder.' Smart's attorney, Paul Twomey, did his best to rebut Pamela's secretly recorded statements. He portrayed Smart as 'a stressed-out basket case' under the care of a psychiatrist. He claimed that his client was emotionally wrecked by her husband's death when she made the taped statements to her former student aide and that she was acting irrationally and taking the anti-depressant,

Prozac. Both of Pamela's lawyers tried unsuccessfully to attack Billy Flynn's heart-wrenching testimony and credibility and accused Cecelia Pierce of protecting Flynn and the other boys at Pamela's expense. During the summation, the crucifix that dangled from Pamela's neck throughout the trial appeared to symbolize the cross that the prosecution had nailed her to.

THE JURY'S VERDICT

The jury of seven women and five men needed only 13 hours of deliberation to return a guilty verdict and ruled that behind Pamela Smart's cool exterior lurked a cunning killer whose cold-bloodedness made her the brains behind her husband's death. 'Her coldness was very striking', said juror Charlotte Jefts. The most damning evidence were the tape recordings that Cecelia Pierce provided to the police. 'The tapes proved in our minds that she was guilty', said juror Norma Honor. The jurors agreed with the prosecution's analysis that Smart 'got her hooks so deep into the hormones of Flynn', that the boy couldn't resist her influence.

'Pamela Smart. I am required and do hereby sentence you to the New Hampshire State prison for women for the remainder of your life without the possibility of parole', stated Judge Douglas R Gray who imposed the mandatory sentence for an accomplice to first-degree murder. A reporter covering the trial wrote, 'She stood quietly, her chin thrust defiantly forward, eyes dry, nails polished, a crucifix around her neck.' Another wrote, 'Labelled the Ice Maiden by the media during her two-and-a-half-week trial, the 23-year-old former high school teacher showed no emotion Friday as a jury found her guilty of conspiring to murder her husband last May so she could pursue her love affair with her teenage killer.'

With the pronouncement of the guilty verdicts, Gregg's parents, who were holding hands with family members in the front row of the Exeter courtroom, erupted into shrieks of joy. Gregg's father, Bill Smart, faced Pam in court and said, 'I pray this is the absolute last time my family and I have to look at your face. You're a cold-blooded murderer . . . a non-caring, non-loving person who deserves to spend the rest of her life in prison.' Bill Smart told the media, 'There's no doubt in my mind or anyone who listened to the tape's mind that she was the one that manipulated, instrumented and proceeded to kill our son.'

NOT GUILTY

Pamela's father, John Wojas, now a retired airline pilot, was stunned by the verdict. 'We try to think back through all her childhood years, if we could ever see a mean streak in her . . . She was the most loveable, friendly kid.' Pamela's mother, Linda Wojas, had her own theory about the verdict, 'I believe it was a moral decision that she made . . . a very poor moral decision when she had the affair but that came back to haunt her. People in New Hampshire shook their finger at her and said, "How dare her?" . . . she was a teacher. She had a nice family. She had a good job. How dare her?' To raise funds for her daughter's legal expenses and a new trial, Linda Wojas started an organization called Friends Of Pamela Smart. She is lobbying the state and federal government, appearing on TV talk shows, organizing prayer vigils outside the prison gates and delivering the message that her daughter 'was tried and convicted in a 20th century witch hunt'.

Pamela insists she is behind bars for a crime she didn't commit. 'I truly wish that I would've been sentenced to death versus sentenced to life without parole because in the death sentence, a person on death row at least has an end in sight.'

Pamela's lawyers have taken her case to the US Supreme Court claiming that their client didn't get a fair trial because of the media blitz and because the jury was not sequestered. Letters written by Flynn and Latimme in prison may prove that they acted without her knowledge and that Pamela was framed by the boys. J.R. Latimme wrote, 'We had no choice: her or us.' So far, the courts have refused to hear Pamela's case.

PRISONER NUMBER 93G 0356

For security reasons, Pamela Smart was transferred from the New Hampshire State prison for women to Bedford Hills prison for women in Westchester County, New York. Because of her notoriety and star status, she was classified as a 'tracker' which meant that her every move would be monitored within the prison. Pamela, who had attended the best schools and lived a comfortable suburban middle-class life, was suddenly cast into a concrete purgatory with hard-boiled drug dealers, thieves, prostitutes, murderers and homeless illiterates. A husky prison guard checked her into her eight by 15-foot single occupancy cell equipped with the bare necessities – toilet, sink, bed and night table. Pamela's eyes scanned the cell. Not exactly a bed and breakfast for vacationing tourists. It was more of a 'cot and chow' for convicted felons who would break her legs, slit her throat and mop the floor with her hair for looking at them the wrong way. Pamela taped a photograph of her dead husband, Gregg, on the concrete wall next to her bed.

Lesbian liaisons in women's prisons are a fact of life and Bedford Hills is no exception. Home-made dildos are made by taking a handful of napkins, ravelling an ace bandage around them and securing them in place with the finger of a rubber glove pulled down over the top. With the arrival of a sexy, young, celebrity school teacher, female suitors jockeyed for first turn. One woman prisoner who claimed to have sexually conquered the criminal superstar, was quoted as saying, 'Pam is insatiable. She openly boasts about her sexual appetite. We call women like her animals because they fuck whenever they feel like it with whoever takes their fancy.' Pamela, who had a distinct preference for African American women, learned the hard way about two strictly enforced prison rules – no snitching and no cheating on lovers. Thirty-two-year-old Mona Graves (serving 20 years to life for murder) and 28-year-old Ghania Miller (serving seven years to life for cocaine possession) blamed Pamela for writing a 'snitch' letter to the prison superintendent and splitting them up. Mona and Ghania decided to turn the tabloid star's face into spaghetti . . . but all in good time.

Pamela complained to the media that 'the only way I'll get out of here is on appeal or in a casket . . . Right now, I hate to even think about it, but it looks like I will leave in a casket.' Cecelia Pierce, her ex-friend and confidante, had driven the spikes into her coffin and sealed it shut. When Pamela heard the news that Cecelia sold her story to a Hollywood producer for $100,000, she allegedly tried to put out a contract on her from behind bars.

While Pamela's lawyers worked on an appeal for a new trial, they advised their client to behave herself. Pamela joined a self-help group for long termers and started working as a teacher's aide at the prison school. She even got a scholarship from the University of Alabama to study criminal justice by correspondence. Her Friends Of Pamela Smart fan club and her daily fan mail became a source of moral support. On 28 October, 1998, while Pamela was taking a smoke break outside the prison school building, the 'Enemies of Pamela Smart' made their move. Ghania Miller, who was doing time for murder, snuck up behind Pamela and leaped on her back like a rabid monkey while Ghania's lesbian lover, Mona, punched, kicked, beat and ground her into hamburger meat. An eyewitness was quoted as saying, 'As they started kicking Pam, she tried to get up and one of them ripped her T-shirt off exposing her breasts . . . one of them grabbed her nipples and dug her nails in hard . . .' During the beating, Pam recalls, 'I could hear her [Ghania] say, "Whip her fucking ass, Mona! Kill that bitch!"' Pamela heard the jingle of a guard's keys in the distance and the next thing she remembers, she was in the prison infirmary with injuries to her head, face, legs and knees. Her left eye socket was fractured and would require the surgical insertion of a plastic plate. Mona and Ghania, were hustled into solitary and charged with assault.

When the news media got wind of the savage beating, Pamela Smart was back in the spotlight again. She testified before a jury for three days against her lesbian attackers. 'For some reason, they thought I wrote a letter about their friendship. The officials admitted they didn't get a letter so all this stupidity is for nothing.' Pamela added, 'Just because I'm incarcerated doesn't mean I'm going to be intimidated and lose whatever dignity I have left.' Mona and Ghania's defense lawyers insisted that Pamela Smart, who seduced and persuaded a young boy to blow her husband's brains out, couldn't be trusted or believed. The prosecutor argued that, 'Pamela Smart was not sentenced to be assaulted at Bedford Hills'. The jury found both Graves and Miller guilty of second-degree assault. As five extra years were added to their prison terms, Miller collapsed into loud sobs and shrieks while Graves showed no emotion. Pamela returned to her cell and pasted photographs, newspaper and magazine clippings from the new publicity into her celebrity scrapbook.

DADDY'S GIRLS

The Mary Letourneau and Pamela Smart stories share striking similarities. Both women are petite, attractive, stylish and energetic. Both were 'daddy's girls', honour-roll students, college educated and came from advantaged backgrounds. Both were teachers with failing marriages who committed statutory rape with an underage male student whom they claimed to be in love with. Both served hard time in women's prisons on opposite sides of the continent.

Unlike Letourneau, Smart initiated the sexual seduction of her student and there is convincing evidence to suggest that the seduction was premeditated and motivated by an intent to exploit the boy as an instrument of murder. In spite of Pamela and Billy's steamy affair and mutual declarations of love, they were both quick to blame one another for Gregg's murder to save their own skins. Asking someone to commit murder or 'committing murder for someone who asks' is not, by most people's standards, an expression of love. Pamela Smart may have been guilty of a lot of things but loving either her husband or her student lover was not one of them. If Pamela Smart had loved Greggory Smart or Billy Flynn half as much as her shih-tzu, Halen, she'd probably have a lot more say about when she gets up in the morning, showers, eats and goes to bed at night.

'It's ironic', says Joyce Maynard, author of *To Die For*. Pamela's driving ambition to become a TV celebrity came true beyond her wildest expectations. She got her photos in all the major newspapers and tabloid magazines. Hollywood even made a movie about her. 'In spite of the tragedy,' says Maynard, 'You have to get a kick out of that.'

5

LIVING DOLL

'Men aren't attracted to me by my mind.
They're attracted by what I don't mind.'
Gypsy Rose Lee

'And so it came to pass that a sex toy who looked like a German
streetwalker has influenced our vision of women', says M.G.
Lord, author of *Forever Barbie*. According to Lord's research
findings, Barbie has X-rated roots and started life as 'Lilli', a
German sex doll from the 1950s. Promoted as the perfect
princess archetype, Barbie still walks on her tippy-toes and
parades her transvestite figure – broad shoulders, Baywatch
breasts, anorexic thin hips and spider long legs. Children all
over the world have been playing with 'a pornographic carica-
ture and a gag gift for men'. Developmentally immature little
girls who play with the ex-sex doll and compare themselves to
her 'streetwalker' image never measure up and never win. Even
her perfectly handsome boyfriend Ken is a perfectly impossible
male ideal.

Cindy Jackson, who imprinted on Barbie's image at age six,
became so obsessed with measuring up to the doll's image that
she devoted her life to it. 'I looked at this doll and her glamorous life and her glamorous clothes and I thought there was a
parallel symbol of womanhood that I was very attached to and

I wanted it.' Becoming a real Barbie cost her seven years of her life, 22 cosmetic surgeries and $55,000 – and she still didn't measure up.

Karla Homolka was another casualty of Barbie obsession. She owned twelve flawless sets of Barbie and Ken dolls and played with them endlessly in her perfect world of make-believe. She fantasized about the real house and the real husband she'd have someday – a real living doll like Ken.

KARLA'S OBSESSION

Other than a mischievous habit of reciting 'cuss' words and an insatiable obsession over Barbie and Ken, Karla Homolka's childhood, according to most accounts, wasn't the kind of childhood you'd expect of a serial sex killer. The Homolkas were a traditional, close-knit family. Karla's father, Karel, a Czech immigrant with broken English, sold black velvet portraits of Elvis and mulatto girls outside shopping malls in St Catherines, a small Ontario town near Niagara Falls. Because of Karel's unpredictable income, the family was forced to live in modest apartments and trailer parks. After Karla was born, her mother, Dorothy, quit her job at the Shaver medical clinic and became a full-time housewife. She gave birth to two more girls, Lori Priscilla and Tammy Lyn. Karel finally found steady work as a travelling salesman and by 1978, he qualified for a mortgage on a comfortable split-level home with a swimming pool.

Karla's silky blond locks and pink frilly dresses gave her an uncanny resemblance to the Barbie dolls she played with so indulgently. Renya, an early school chum at Parnell public school, approached her one day and asked her, 'Are you a princess?' The two girls became best friends even though Renya didn't share Karla's playtime obsession for pretend dolls and a pretend world. Karla was very possessive over her dolls and Renya started to get concerned about her when she was still playing 'let's pretend' with the dolls at age 14. Renya didn't have the heart to ask, 'Aren't you getting way too old for that, Karla?'

GOING OVERBOARD

The boys swarmed around Karla Homolka like restless zoo animals at feeding time. She was one of the hottest looking girls at Winston Churchill High. Besides having the figure and face of a Baywatch blond, she was also brainy and had one of the highest IQ's in the school. Karla joined the choir, the school dance club and took up gymnastics and figure skating. In a sudden and dramatic turnabout Karla traded in her 'preppiness' for 'evilness' and embraced witchcraft, demons, curses and death.

Like a typical teenager, Karla rebelled against her parents' authority by making a loud fashion statement. She teased and colored her honey blond locks into an electric shock look and swapped her feminine frills for trendy rags. To go with her shocking punk image, Karla needed a shocking punk philosophy like 'ugly is cool', 'no pain, no gain', 'screw your neighbour', 'life's a bitch' and 'God's a slob'. Karla decided that 'God didn't really exist . . . but there was a devil, an evil in the world that people worshipped'. Horror flicks like *Friday The 13th* became Karla's new truth. Blood, guts and gore became her passion. She told a friend, 'You know what I'd like to do? I'd like to put dots all over somebody's body and take a knife and then play connect the dots and then pour vinegar all over them.'

Karla was getting lots of mileage out of her punk fashions and occult hobbies but she could just as easily have attracted the same attention with a T-shirt that said, 'Look at me. I'm different.'

Karla wasn't really all that different from any other trend conforming teeny-bopper – except that she went overboard. Whether it was Barbie dolls, punk rock, the occult, kinky sex or murder, Karla went overboard with everything she did.

Iona Brindle remembered seeing strange carved circles on Karla's arms that were filled in with nail polish. Karla once gave Iona a book, *Michele Remembers*, about a victim's true story of sexual abuse and satanic ritual. Inside the book she wrote, 'There is always something more left to say.' She showed another friend some scars where she'd superficially cut her wrists with a knife. 'I tried to kill myself,' she confided. 'Sometimes I just don't want to live.'

Family arguments often flared up when Karla's father hit the bottle. Karla would call him a 'dumb Czech' and tell him to 'fuck off'. But her father's drinking wasn't the only problem plaguing the Homolka house. Karel had a roving eye and made amorous advances towards Lynda Wollis at the Shaver medical clinic where his wife, Dorothy, used to work. Women at the clinic nicknamed Karel 'the pervert'. Dorothy, who had ballooned into a stocky middle-aged housewife, cared for her marriage and approached her friend, Lynda, with a kinky proposition – 'You could save my marriage if you'd sleep with both of us', she pleaded. Lynda declined. At 17, Karla was anxious to move out of the house and live on her own. She bought bridal magazines and fantasized about her 'special day', her 'special man', and her 'special house'. She could hardly wait. By grade twelve, she landed a full time job at the Number One Pet Center and took only two high school courses that year.

A LIVING DOLL

On 17 October 1987, Karla and her sidekick, Debbie, turned

up at a pet industry convention at the Howard Johnson Hotel in a Scarborough suburb near Toronto. After a night on the town, the girls returned to the hotel and found a couple of pets on-the-make in their hotel coffee shop. One of them was Paul Bernardo. Karla's heart turned somersaults. He was 23, 6 foot 1, 180 pounds with blond wavy hair, dreamy blue eyes, a dimpled pretty boy face – and his middle name was 'Ken' just like the doll – except Paul was a real doll. Paul was a living doll. Paul was the man she knew she would marry someday. She knew it the minute she laid eyes on him.

Karla hardly even noticed Paul's buddy, Van Smirnis. Even though she thought of herself as 'an old fashioned kind of girl', Karla threw caution to the wind and invited the pair up to her hotel room to watch a movie. Paul and Van exchanged victory smiles. They couldn't believe their luck.

Van and Debbie, were an obvious mismatch. They sat and watched Paul and Karla exchange mating calls for four straight hours. In the heat of passion, Karla cooed, 'You're beautiful. I love you.' The next morning, the sleepless lovers exchanged phone numbers.

When Karla got back home to St Catherine's, she phoned her friend, Renya, and told her she'd met 'the most perfect man in the whole world' – a gorgeous looking, University of Toronto grad from Scarborough. After listening to Karla gush and drool over her new beau, Renya remarked, 'I think Barbie just met Ken.'

The following weekend, Paul drove two and half hours from Scarborough to St Catherine's to see Karla. They went to a horror movie, *Prince of Darkness*, on their first date. After the movie, Karla brought her perfect man back to her basement bedroom where she whipped out a set of handcuffs, got down on her knees and cuffed her wrists behind her back. She asked Paul to lift up her skirt. Paul preferred women who didn't ask for it – like the women strangers who he'd sexually assaulted at night in his home town of Scarborough. Paul asked Karla how she'd feel if he was a rapist. 'Cool', she murmured.

Karla's parents were social butterflies who hosted barbecue parties and entertained by their pool. They welcomed Paul into their home and offered him a couch to sleep on. He was educated, had a good job as an accountant at Price Waterhouse and appeared to have a shining future. The entire family was charmed by his polite, innocent manner and generosity. He'd bring wine and gifts on his visits and soon became the Homolka's 'weekend son'. During sleepovers, Paul would wait until Karla's parents turned in for the night, then he'd sneak into Karla's bedroom, bang her all night long and return to the couch before dawn. Karla was head over heels in love with him. 'He was the one guy who was very nice to me; he never bored me like the others. With the other guys, I could always do what I wanted and that was boring. In all my previous relationships, I was in total control. I never cared what others thought.'

Between visits, Paul sent flowers. Karla wrote cards and letters. 'To my prince – love from your princess' and 'Roses are red, violets are blue, there's nothing more fun than a pervert like you.' In another note, she wrote, 'Paul – I love you. Please don't stop loving me . . . Tomorrow and forever, I love you . . . Don't rip off all my clothes and ravish me like a beast for a solid hour. Do it all night . . . '

Paul called Karla his 'little princess'. That Christmas, he gave his little princess a $300 dress, a gold necklace, a watch and a teddy bear. Karla gave her king an authentic looking gift certificate that said, 'Karla Leanne Homolka will perform sick,

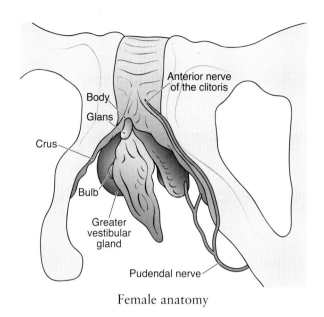

Female anatomy

John Bobbitt points during testimony in the sixth day
of Lorena Bobbitt's sexual abuse trial against him

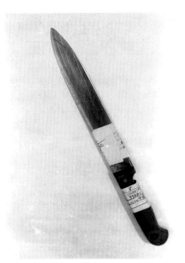

The knife used by Lorena Bobbitt to cut off the penis of her husband, John Bobbitt, is part of the evidence used in her malicious wounding trial

John Bobbitt's severed penis

Lorena Bobbitt, flanked by her attornies James Lowe, *left*, and Lisa Kemler, meets reporters outside court in Manassas, Virginia. A judge ordered her release from a mental hospital, five weeks after her acquittal on reason of insanity for cutting off her husband's penis

Vili Fualaau with his lawyer Bob Huff

Mary Kay Letourneau in court, hearing that
she must complete her six-month sentence

Pamela and Gregg Smart on their wedding day

Pamela Smart

William Flynn, the young man who Pamela
seduced and coerced into killing her husband

Karla Homolka, Lori Homolka and father Karel Homolka

Paul Bernardo in a police car

A salesman watches an interview with Karla Homolka on television station RDI in Montreal, 4 July 2005

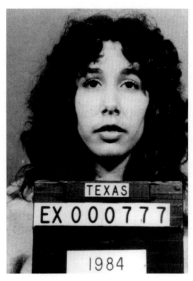

Karla Faye Tucker

Melchora Vasquez, chief clerk
for Harris County's trial
exhibits, returns the pickaxe
used by condemned killer Karla
Faye Tucker in the 1983 killing
of Jerry Lynn Dean

'That'll learn ya!'
George W. Bush

perverted acts upon Paul Kenneth Bernardo. These acts may be chosen by the recipient of the coupon.' As part of the Yuletide fun, the couple rented Karla's favorite movie – a film called *Criminal Law* about a serial rapist (Kevin Bacon) who rapes young women, stuffs disposable diapers in their mouths, strangles and kills them, then lights their genitals on fire to destroy the forensic evidence.

Eleven rapes had been reported to the police by women in the Scarborough area. The knife-wielding attacker dubbed 'The Scarborough Rapist', had reportedly forced his victims to say 'I love you' while he raped them.

PAUL 'KEN' BERNARDO

When Paul was born, his mother screamed at the sight of him. He had a large ugly black splotch covering the left side of his head. The inky splotch vanished six weeks later and turned out to be a transient blood clot. Paul was incoherent until five years of age. Instead of talking, he pointed and grunted like a chimp. The doctors discovered that his tongue was attached to the roof of his mouth by a bizarre flange of skin that looked like the webbing on a duck's foot. Once the webbing was snipped, Paul spoke with a speech impediment which was later corrected with the help of a speech therapist.

The Bernardo family lived in an upper-middle-class neighbourhood of Scarborough. Paul's father, Ken Bernardo, was a religious church-going family man and a professional accountant who wore thick coke bottle glasses perched on the bridge of his nose. He believed women should be kept in their place and earned a reputation with his neighbours as a wife beater, child molester (including an incestuous relationship with his own daughter) and a 'Peeping Tom'. The Bernardos kept to themselves but screams and family rows were audible to the next-door neighbours. Paul's father was caught molesting a nine-year-old girl and was charged with sexual assault.

Like his role model, Paul developed a taste for voyeurism and pubescent girls in his mid-teens. He collected clippings from store catalogues of girl models posing in brassiere and underwear ads. At night, he'd hide behind bushes and peep through windows at naked girls. He later graduated to hard core X-rated master-slave videos that he bought or rented from Toronto's downtown video stores. Watching women suffering and being brutally raped, sodomized and tied up aroused him to climax. His perverse sado-masochistic interests extended to defecating and urinating on women and other lewd acts involving domination, pain, degradation and the humiliation of women and girls. He even got his hands on underground kiddie porn and some home-made 'raised skirt' videos.

Paul's mother, Marilyn, was outlandish, flabby, drab, untidy, foul-mouthed and loud. Besides having psychiatric and drinking problems, Marilyn had wild mood swings. An underactive thyroid gland caused her skin and hair to dry out and made her obese. Like some hideous giant troll, she moved into the dimly lit basement of the house, stopped feeding the kids and began hiding her food. Paul hated her. He called her a 'slob', a 'fucking cunt', a 'big fat cow', a 'whore' and an 'it'. His anger towards his mother and towards women generally was fuelled by a traumatic incident that occurred when he was sixteen. During one of Marilyn's violent mood swings, she told Paul that he was a 'bastard from hell' and that Ken Bernardo wasn't his real father. She showed him a photograph of an ex-boyfriend who she claimed was Paul's real father.

STICKS AND STONES

Karla had a pet name for Paul's penis. She called it 'Snuffles'. As winter ushered in spring, Snuffles was having a hard time climaxing. Karla's efforts to be sexually more aggressive weren't working. Paul demanded that she start calling herself filthy names while she blew him. He reminded her that she wasn't a virgin which entitled him to 'do it up the ass.' When Karla objected, he sulked and muttered, 'I deserved a virgin. I don't love you any more.'

Karla broke out in shingles, a stress-related skin rash. Fearing she might pass it on to him, Paul hit the road and headed back to Scarborough. Karla wrote him a letter of apology. 'I'm sorry for what I've done . . . I hate myself. I know I don't deserve it, but I want a second chance. Hearing you say you didn't love me was one of the worst days of my life. I guess I really screwed things up. There are no perfect people in this world. One day, you may find your virgin.' In a follow-up letter, she said, 'I also want to apologize for my stupid insecurities . . . I wish to God I wasn't such a stupid idiot. Sometimes I feel just so useless. Please let's not fight again.' She signed it, 'Your furry little creature, Karly Curls.'

When Karla agreed to submit to anal sex, Paul zoomed back to St Catherine's faster than the road-runner. Whenever they had sex after that, Karla would ritually say, 'I'm your little cocksucker, I'm your little cunt. I'm your little slut.' In a greeting card, she wrote, 'Sticks and stones may break my bones/but whips and chains excite me/only you know how much.' In another note, she wrote, 'You're such a disgusting sexual pervert. I love that in a man', and 'the power you wield over me is indescribable . . . with you in my life, I feel complete. With you in my life, nothing can go wrong . . . I love you forever no matter what.'

In the summer of 1988, Karla and Paul flew off on a ten-day trip to Florida's Disney World and nestled in at the Marriott. They bought mouse ears and hammed it up in front of Paul's home video camera. That same summer, the happy 'mouse-keteers' moved into Paul's house in Scarborough while his parents were away on vacation. For recreation, they re-enacted scenes from porn movies. Paul tied a black electrical cord around Karla's neck, pressed a knife to the side of her head and had anal sex with her. Karla choked and clawed and gasped for air as Paul yanked at the cord and recited porn movie lines – 'Get your ass in the air . . . arch your back'. It was a torturous experience that triggered flashbacks of the asthma attacks that Karla experienced as a child. After nearly strangling to death, Karla smiled and posed as Paul took sixteen kinky photographs of her gagged and handcuffed with a wine bottle inserted into her vagina. He took shots of her nipples and genitals covered in whipping cream and shots of rectal intercourse and fellatio – the kind of shots that would interest porn dealers.

LORD AND MASTER

Paul delighted in testing new sexual limits. He asked Karla to wear a dog collar during sex. When she called the idea stupid, he hauled off and hit her for the very first time but he quickly apologized. He didn't apologize the next time. Karla gave in and bought a dog collar. She also bought a picture of a dog and wrote on it, 'He's just like the dog that I am – the fucking dog.' At Paul's urging, she wrote reminders to herself about how stupid she was. She wrote and taped the reminders to her bedroom door. 'Remember, you're stupid. Remember to think before you speak.' Comparing herself to the perfect Barbie dolls she'd played with as a child, Karla was imperfect. Paul made that fact perfectly clear to her. Because she didn't measure up, he ordered her to start a 'self improvement' list.

- Never let anyone know our relationship is anything but perfect
- Don't talk back to Paul
- Always smile when you're with Paul
- Be a perfect girlfriend for Paul
- If Paul asks for a drink, bring him one quickly and happily
- Remember you're stupid
- Remember you're ugly
- Remember you're fat
- I don't know why I tell you these things because you never change

Paul was an immaculate, expensive and trendy dresser. He started highlighting his hair and aimed for the All-American beach-boy look. Like an idol-worshipping teenager, Karla filled every inch of her bedroom and dresser with photos of Paul. Her friends were surprised when she changed her wardrobe and hair to the high school 'preppie' image that she used to hate. She even changed her diet to please Paul. Whenever she spoke, instead of saying 'I' or 'we', she'd parrot Paul's opinions. Paul this. Paul that. She talked non-stop about what Paul was doing, what Paul was thinking and what Paul was saying.

Beside her bed, Karla hung a dog collar, handcuffs and ribbons. Paul liked her to wear the ribbons in her hair when they had sex so she'd look like an innocent school-girl. He'd pretend to be a 'big bad businessman' and she'd pretend to be his worshipping young virgin. When he ordered her to swallow his semen, she dutifully obliged. In her notes to him, she wrote, 'I'm your little cocksucker, cunt, slut, asslicker and I want to marry you . . . your wish is my command.'

Karla's friends finally met the dreamboat hunk that Karla had been raving about for so long. Instead of the gorgeous centerfold that she had described to them, they met a giggling goof with a baby-fat face, vacant eyes and a-holier-than-thou 'attitude'. They accepted him only because Karla said he spoiled her and treated her like a princess. As time wore on, Karla saw less and less of her friends and told them not to phone her when Paul was away because it pissed him off when he called her and got a busy signal. 'I live for the weekend. It's like I'm dead during the week', she told them.

For her 4 May birthday, Paul gave Karla a 'promise ring'. It symbolized his promise to dictate what she wore, who she saw, what she said and what they did. He was her lord, master and owner. She was his obedient sex slave who must account for every waking moment away from him. To keep this dangerous, sexy man in her life, Karla was game to do anything and everything her lord and master asked.

VIRGIN FARM

Paul's fantasy from the time he was a teenager was to have his own virgin farm of young schoolgirls whose only purpose in life would be to sexually service him and obey his every wish. Paul viewed females as something to be used, dominated, manipulated, abused and controlled. He told his friend, Van Smirnis, about his basic philosophy in life – that it was a cruel dog-eat-dog world, that vulnerable human beings, especially women, existed for the purpose of being consumed and used by men who were the more powerful of the species. To Paul, a woman was just a weak creature living in the jungle – a creature to be exploited.

Paul boasted to Van Smirnis that he had Karla 'dancing on a string'. He described how she'd dress up like a schoolgirl in pigtails and get down on her knees for him. He flaunted gift certificates on his dresser. 'This certificate hereby certifies that Karla Leanne Homolka loves Paul Kenneth Bernardo with all her heart and soul and will follow him wherever.' Paul confessed that he was totally wired – but not for Karla. He was wired for the virginal flesh of Karla's younger sister, Tammy. He told Van he liked to wrestle and play with the 14-year-old while Karla watched and seethed with jealousy. Tammy would say to him, 'I'm more pretty than Karla, ain't I?' and Paul would answer, 'Of course you are.'

TO HAVE AND TO HOLD

Karla lost her job at the Thorold Veterinary Clinic after the veterinarian suspected her of stealing an animal sedative. She landed another job almost immediately at the Martindale Animal Clinic where she was placed in charge of the drug registry. Although Karla had been accepted at the University of Toronto, her all-consuming ambition in life was to become Mrs Paul Bernardo. She abandoned her studies and dedicated herself to that task.

Paul quit his job at Price Waterhouse to pursue a more lucrative career – smuggling cigarettes from the United States into Canada. He'd pay 10 bucks a carton in the US and sell them in Canada at twenty-five bucks a carton. Paul bought a $4,500 wedding ring with his contraband earnings, slipped it on Karla's finger and asked her to marry him. She was so elated, she wanted to shout it from the rooftops. The man Karla worshipped with every atom of her being asked her to be his wife. She wrote to a Toronto newspaper and described the monumental occasion. 'The most romantic moment of my life occurred on December 9th', she wrote. 'My wonderful boyfriend of five years – Paul – took me on a romantic walk to the romance capitol of the world, Niagara Falls. We walked hand-in-hand alongside the majestic falls. It was a lover's paradise that evening, with red and green Christmas lights all along the falls. Softly falling snow, and other romantic couples strolling in the soft moonlight. As we approached the elf-sized Christmas village, Paul told me he had a gift for me. I turned my back at his request. He pulled out a box containing a glass unicorn music box. Perched across the unicorn's horn was a perfect diamond ring. As we waited for some noisy children to leave, he whispered words of love in my ear and hugged me tightly in an effort to keep us warm – it was very cold and windy. Finally the children left and we were alone outside of the elves' church . . . '

IF YOU REALLY LOVE ME

The wedding was scheduled for 29 June 1991. Karla raved to her friends about her god-like fiancé. 'He'll make the perfect husband. I can't wait 'til it's official'. The wedding meant everything to Karla. It would be a wedding fit for royalty with a horse and carriage and all the trimmings – exactly as she'd imagined it since childhood. Nothing would stand in the way of her special day with her special man – nothing except her 14-year-old sister, Tammy Lyn.

In July of 1990, Tammy Lynn left the house with Paul on a twenty-minute errand. Twenty minutes turned into six hours. Karla was steaming mad when they got back and demanded an explanation but none was offered. Paul later told her he was bored with his sex life. He wanted a threesome. If she wasn't into it, then she could kiss the wedding and their relationship goodbye. Karla asked him who he had in mind. 'Tammy', he replied. 'If you were a good enough girlfriend, I wouldn't need Tammy.' Karla argued that Tammy wouldn't know what to do with 'Snuffles'. The argument escalated and Karla slapped him across the face for the first time. Paul beat her senseless until she apologized.

Hoping Paul would eventually tire of his interest in her pubescent sister, Karla continued with her wedding plans. Planning the perfect wedding was time consuming. The bridesmaids had to be measured. The service, the reception and the invitations had to be arranged. It was going to be the biggest, happiest, day of her life and everything had to be perfect.

Instead of waning, Paul's obsession with Tammy intensified. He wanted to be the first and he wanted Karla's cooperation. He tried guilt trips – since Karla couldn't give him her own virginity, he deserved her sister's virginity. He tried reasoning with her – better him than some horny young buck from Tammy's school. He tried begging – 'If you really love me . . . let me do it to Tammy'. He even tried bribing her and put a deposit down on her cinderella style wedding gown. Karla agreed to a compromise plan. That evening at dinner, she crushed up some valium tablets and sprinkled them on Tammy's spaghetti. Later that night, Paul snuck into the girl's room while she was in a drugged stupor. He stood over her, masturbated and ejaculated on her pillow. The experience only served to whet his appetite further. Karla knew she had to do something fast and get the situation under control. She tried helping Paul make videos of Tammy undressing at night. She even pretended to be her sister when they had sex together – but nothing satisfied him.

By November 1990, Paul had accumulated $25,000 in credit card debts. He declared personal bankruptcy but kept right on spending with Karla's credit cards. He bought himself a new Sony Camcorder video camera. Shortly before Christmas,

Paul pressed Karla one more time for Tammy's virginity. 'Now this would make a great Christmas present for me.' He assured her that he'd wear a condom, that nobody would get hurt and that Tammy would never know about it.' With a little dose of animal anaesthetic from the vet clinic she'd never know what happened to her.

GUILTY AS SIN

The local newspaper displayed a composite drawing of the suspect dubbed the 'Scarborough Rapist'. Tina Smirnis saw the drawing and called the police. Tina was the sister-in-law of Paul's best friend, Van Smirnis. She and her husband, Alex Smirnis, who had lived across the street from Paul, told the police that Paul Bernardo looked just like the man in the drawing. A couple of detectives called Paul into the sexual assault squad office and interviewed him.

After the police interview, Paul drove to St Catherine's to see Karla. He was visibly shaken. 'I've just been questioned about the Scarborough rapist case,' he told her. 'But you didn't do those rapes,' Karla protested. 'What if they arrest me . . . What if they charge me anyways?' he asked, nervously. 'They took my forensics . . . The police said it would take a month or so to get the forensic results back.' Karla offered to be Paul's alibi if he needed one. 'What if I am the Scarborough rapist?' he finally said, matter-of-factly. Karla tensed. 'Don't, Paul.' He shrugged. 'Maybe I am, maybe I'm not.'

On the anniversary of their engagement, Karla gave Paul a card and covered it with hearts. 'Just for fun I made a list of the top hundred things I like to do with you . . . kiss and hug and stuff: "you know what stuff"'. She signed it, 'W-U-V, Karly Curls'. To reassure Paul of her undying love and devotion, she wrote him a note, 'Please accept my apology even though actions speak louder than words and my actions haven't been great. I swear things will change. Just remember how much we love each other. Paul, I know we can get through this . . . '

THE TIE THAT BINDS

The Sunday before Christmas, Paul videotaped the Homolka family drinking tropical cocktails and celebrating. Fourteen-year-old Tammy sipped a Daiquiri and a Rusty Nail spiked with sedatives. She stayed up to watch a movie with her big sister and her boyfriend after the others went to bed. The movie, called *Lisa and the Devil*, was about a sadist, a nymphomaniac and a necrophiliac.

As Tammy dozed off into a sedated sleep, Karla poured some halothane animal anaesthetic onto a cloth and pressed it over her sister's mouth and nose. 'Please hurry up before somebody comes down,' whispered Karla as Paul unwrapped his Christmas gift. 'Shhh, you're gettin' all worked up,' he complained as he undressed the girl. Karla told him to wear a condom like he'd promised. 'Put it on,' she scolded. When Paul refused, she whispered hoarsely, 'Fucking do it! Just do it!' Paul looked at her and said, 'Do you love me?' He knew that question would shut her up. While the family slept upstairs, Paul videotaped himself taking Tammy's virginity. Karla added more animal anaesthetic to the cloth (six times the recommended dosage for dogs) and covered Tammy's face with it to make sure she didn't wake up. Paul urged Karla to participate. He pointed the video camera at her and zoomed in on her as she pumped her sister's vagina with her fingers, then performed oral sex on her – even though Tammy was menstruating at the time. 'Fucking disgusting', protested

Karla with a blood wet grimace. The comatose girl vomited as Paul began sodomizing her. 'Oh, my god, she's not breathing,' Karla exclaimed in a panic. Paul withdrew and tried unsuccessfully to clear Tammy's throat. 'I think I just killed my sister!' gasped Karla. Paul and Karla dragged the girl's limp and lifeless body into the bedroom and quickly dressed her. As Paul tried mouth to mouth resuscitation, Karla phoned 911, then poured the animal anaesthetic down the sink and hid the pills. When the police arrived, the couple told them that Tammy suddenly stopped breathing while they were watching television. They said they tried to save her with mouth-to-mouth resuscitation.

The autopsy report determined that Tammy Lynn Homolka had died of aspiration or fluid on the lungs, that she had vomited after passing out and in an unconscious state had swallowed enough vomit to choke to death. The coroner neglected to do any blood tests.

At the funeral home, Paul stood by Tammy's coffin and made a farewell gesture. He took the ring off of his finger and slid it onto Tammy's finger. Paul blamed Karla and her 'stupid drugs' for Tammy's death. 'I could tell them [Karla's family] what you did to Tammy and your life would be over,' he warned. Karla justified her actions with, 'I didn't give you my virginity . . . so I gave you Tammy's. I love you enough to do that.'

Karla mistakenly assumed that once Paul had taken her sister's virginity, it would cure his obsession. Instead, he told her to dress up in Tammy's clothes whenever they had sex. 'Paul had something he could hold over me for the rest of my life . . . I was terrified my family would hate me if they ever found out.' Donning her dead sister's underwear, Karla smiled and licked and sucked on cue.

116

'VENUS FLYTRAP'

Like switching television channels, Karla had the uncanny ability to switch back and forth from nightmare reality to fairytale fantasy. On 18 January 1991, Karla and Paul found their dream home at 57 Bayview in Port Dalhousie – later dubbed 'The Venus Flytrap' by lawyer John Rosen. It was a one-and-half storey Cape Cod style pink bungalow with skylights and a cedar deck. Paul bought Karla a Rottweiler puppy and called him, 'Buddy'. At last, Karla was getting everything she wanted in life. Paul would soon be her husband and they'd start a family together. She was ecstatic.

People magazine described them as 'a couple so clean-cut that their neighbours in Port Dalhousie called them "Ken and Barbie"'. They were the upwardly mobile couple next door living in a picture-book house in a fashionable neighbourhood – young, prosperous, attractive, self-indulgent, middle class, generation Xers with matching blond hair. Paul even joined the Masons and became an active member of the community.

On 5 April, 1991, Paul didn't come home all night and Karla was worried sick. When he finally showed up the next day, Karla demanded to know where he'd been. 'I just raped a girl,' he said, casually. Paul told her to sleep on the floor from now on. The queen-size bed wasn't big enough for both of them. Karla got some blankets and made a bed for herself on the floor. When she made the mistake of closing the bathroom door while she took a pee, Paul punished her severely. He had trained her never to pee with the door closed. 'Because you're so stupid, be ready for the nightly terror attack' – which meant a beating with his belt, followed by sodomy. Karla wrote Paul a letter of apology. 'I'm so sorry about last night. I love you so much. Please forgive me.' In spite of her apologies and best efforts, the beatings became progressively more routine and violent. Paul stopped needing a reason to beat the daylights out of her and called her 'bitch' and 'cunt' in front of her friends. He told her to get more Halcion from the veterinary clinic in case he brought a girl home. When she returned without the Halcion, he beat her but this time it was different. This time he beat her in visible areas of her body. Karla would wait for the bruises to heal before going back to work.

Karla was desperate. On her twenty-first birthday, she wrote in a letter to Paul, 'You hate me. You say you want to go out with other girls . . . you say I make you sick. You tell me to pack and leave. You tell me to eat shit . . . I want us to be happy like we used to be. I think you hate me too much for that to ever happen.' Karla became even more desperate after viewing an explicit video of one of Paul's sexual infidelities. She knew that unless she doubled her efforts to accommodate his perverse sexual tastes, she would never see her wedding day. Karla promised to help Paul abduct fifty virgins – every weekend if he wanted. 'If you want to do it fifty more times, we'll do it fifty more times.'

On 14 June 1991, Paul was out prowling the streets searching for some licence plates to steal for his cigarette smuggling operation. He saw a 14-year-old girl with braces on her teeth – Leslie Mahaffy. The girl was Paul's type – attractive, idealistic, adventurous and trusting with her whole life ahead of her. Leslie was circling around to the back of the house where she lived with her parents. She checked the back door. It was locked. She noticed a prowler and asked him what he was doing. Paul answered, 'Well, I'm trying to pick a house over there.' Leslie said, 'Cool.' She told him, 'I've been locked out of my house and I'm scared to wake up my parents . . . I don't know where to stay . . . have you got a cigarette?' Paul told her he had some smokes in his car so Leslie followed him. Paul's leased gold 240X Nissan was parked close by. He opened the door, reached under the seat, pulled out a knife and used it to force Leslie into the car. He tossed her a turtleneck sweater and ordered her to pull it over her head as a blindfold. 'Just do what I tell you and you won't get hurt . . . if you try to run, I'll kill you.' Paul drove home with his juvenile prey and pulled into the garage. He got out of the car and steered the blindfolded girl into the house and up to the master bedroom. Paul woke Karla up, got out his home video camera and started video-taping three-way sex with his captive and his fiancée. For two solid days, the couple repeatedly raped, sodomized, degraded and sexually terrorized Leslie Mahaffy recreating scenes and dialogue from their porn movies.

FATHER'S DAY

16 June was Father's Day. Karla and Paul had to get rid of their captive before Karla's parents arrived for Father's Day dinner. Leslie had seen Paul. She could identify him and ruin everything. 'I promise I won't tell anyone. Please let me go,' pleaded Leslie, who was blindfolded throughout the ordeal.

According to Karla's version of events, she gave the girl some sleeping pills and a stuffed animal to hold on to for comfort. Then, Paul went and got a black electrical cord, noosed it around Leslie's neck and strangled her to death. Paul had a different version of the events. He wanted to take the blind-folded girl somewhere near her home town of Burlington and dump her off. While he was in another room getting ready to leave, Karla knelt on top of Leslie's back, held her face into a pillow and suffocated her. Paul and Karla both concurred that after killing the girl, they dragged her naked body down the basement steps, put her in the root cellar, then went back upstairs to start dinner.

Paul and Karla were friendly and upbeat when the Homolka's arrived for Father's Day dinner. Karla's mother, Dorothy, helped in the kitchen and volunteered to fetch some potatoes from the root cellar. Paul quickly intercepted her and sent Karla downstairs instead. The evening went by without a hitch. After the Homolkas left, Paul told Karla about his plan to dispose of Leslie's corpse. He would cut off her legs, arms and head with a circular saw and encase the dismembered parts in Kwikmix cement. Then they would drive to Lake Gibson and throw the cement blocks into the lake.

THE PERFECT WEDDING

Karla was furious. 'My parents are being assholes. They pulled half of the money out of the wedding, saying they can't afford it. Bullshit . . . fuck my parents . . . ', wrote Karla to her friend Debbie. She told Debbie that most of the wedding money had been spent on Tammy's funeral and that her parents couldn't afford to pay for the entire wedding now. Karla reminded her parents that her wedding day was the most important day of her life. There had to be real flowers, a sit-down dinner, champagne, a carriage ride – just like she'd always planned it. Paul suggested that the Homolka's remortgage their house. Bending under pressure, Karla's parents agreed to pay for most of the wedding if Paul's parents would split the rest. To raise more money, Karla and Paul brainstormed an idea. Why not ask their wedding guests to donate money instead of gifts? If the wedding was big enough, they could make a killing.

120

29 June 1991. The wedding day that Karla had been planning her entire lifetime was blessed with sunny blue skies. A white Cadillac limousine delivered the radiant young bride to historic St Mark's church in the picture perfect tourist town of Niagara-On-The-Lake. She was wearing a traditional, white satin, $2,000 Demitrios Cinderella style gown with pinched waist, puff sleeves and a veil adorned with garlands. No one suspected the ugly black bruises hidden beneath the white lace. One hundred and fifty guests crowded into the church pews, fanning themselves with their wedding programs to combat the midday heat.

At the Corinthian decorated altar, Paul 'Ken' Bernardo stood poised like a fashion model with his dimpled cherubic face, wavy blond hair and expensive tuxedo. Prior to the ceremony, he reminded Karla that he was only marrying her because 'a wife can't testify against her husband'. Karla pretended not to hear him. All eyes were upon her now as her father delivered her to the man of her dreams. The minister opened the wedding ceremony with, 'We have come together in this place of God . . . ' and closed with, 'May your marriage home be one of truth, security and love.'

In a hailstorm of confetti, the jubilant newlyweds fled from the church and stepped up into the white horse drawn carriage that awaited them out front. Karla's childhood friend, Renya, was among the well-wishers. She smiled at Karla and silently mouthed, 'Congratulations, Barbie.' The bride and groom basked in the sunlight and sipped champagne as the horse drawn carriage clippity-clopped along the bay. They waved like royalty to well-wishers who saw no trace of unbridled evil in their carefree, youthful faces. For Tammy Homolka and Leslie Mahaffy, there would never be a wedding day or any other day.

THE PERFECT RECEPTION

Marilyn Bernardo looked like she'd spent the night under the freeway. She sat chewing on a wad of gum in her massive, wrinkled mauve dress, marinating in sweat from the afternoon humidity. When she discovered the entrée for the sit-down dinner was pheasant stuffed with veal, she stormed over to Paul dragging a white cast on one leg and glared at him. 'I can't believe you got pheasant! I can't eat bird! I can only eat meat! You got this just to bother me!' she screeched. Table guests gasped as Paul gave his mother the finger and said, 'Fuck you, mom. Fuck you! Sit down and eat your fucking meal!'

The bridesmaids were abuzz . . . and so was the gossip as the couple posed for photographs and sliced open a three-tiered white wedding cake topped with plastic bride and groom figures. Karla's father stood at the microphone, raised his glass and toasted to his deceased daughter, Tammy. The bride quickly switched channels and toasted to her new husband. 'Most of all, I'd like to thank my husband for making this the happiest day of my life,' Karla chirped. A friend of Paul's stood up and made a toast to his buddy. 'It's a good thing that Karla works at a vet's and loves animals because that's what she's marrying.' The giggling bride and groom waltzed onto the dance floor to 'Unchained Melody' and 'you never close your eyes any more when I kiss your lips.'

MEANWHILE . . .

Only twenty miles from the wedding ceremony, a father and his son were fishing in Lake Gibson. They noticed some very odd-looking cement sculptures protruding from the water, so they waded over to investigate.

THE PERFECT WEDDING NIGHT

Three bottles of champagne awaited them at their hotel room overlooking the bay at Niagara-On-The-Lake. The honey-mooners would fly off to Hawaii the next day for a blissful honeymoon vacation. That night, Karla slipped into a sheer negligee and flaunted herself. When she failed to get Paul's attention as he drank champagne in front of the TV set, she resorted to negative attention by calling herself 'cunt', 'cocksucker' and 'slut' in the wrong order. Paul had trained her to call herself a 'cocksucker' first, then a 'cunt' and a 'slut'. He forced Karla to apologize. She got her insults in the right order and was permitted to sleep on the bed that night.

THE PERFECT HONEYMOON

They went to Maui, frolicked in the sun and sand, island hopped and videotaped their magic moments together. 'The beauty of this ocean, this beach, and everything here does not come close to equalling the love I feel for you, sweetheart,' scribbled Karla onto an empty sheet of paper.

THE EVER AFTER

When the honeymooners returned home from Hawaii, the entire town of St Catherine's was animated with talk of murder. Karla's parents updated the couple on the latest developments. The police had puzzled together the cemented torso, limbs and head of a 14-year-old Burlington girl, Leslie Mahaffy, who was found in Lake Gibson. Karla and Paul couldn't believe their ears. They'd gone to such great lengths to dispose of the girl's body. What could possibly have gone wrong? When Paul found out that Lake Gibson had fluctuating water levels, he blamed Karla. She was from the area. She should have known about it.

The honeymoon was over. Karla wrote letters to all of her friends telling them how blissfully happy she was. She talked about how much she loved Paul and how much she wanted his baby. On 1 October, she wrote a letter to Paul, 'We are the perfect couple . . . some couples are meant to be and we're one of those . . . Please honey, let's try and have a fairytale marriage like we were meant to . . . I know what happened to us is all my fault and believe me, I'm changing. I love you too much to lose you.'

In August, Karla returned home with a naive 15-year-old virgin, 'Jane Doe', who she met while working at the Number One pet store. Jane had a crush on Karla and Karla took advantage of that crush by feeding Jane to the beast. Paul compared Jane to Tammy. He bought her expensive gifts, wined and dined her and took her to see *Phantom Of The Opera*. Jane watched videos, listened to music and made out with the couple. Feeling like a third wheel in the threesome, Paul decided Jane wasn't being cooperative enough for his taste. He told her, 'If you want to stay friends with Karla, you will suck my dick.' Unhappy with the girl's performance, Paul and Karla gave the girl Halcion and videotaped group sex with her while she was comatose. After almost losing her to an overdose, they managed to resuscitate her. Jane eventually clued in to the obvious. Karla didn't love her and was only using her to service her pathetic husband. The girl left and never came back.

In December 1991, Paul Bernardo's sister, Debbie, laid sexual assault charges against her father, Ken Bernardo. She caught him sexually molesting her four-year-old daughter the same way he'd molested her when she was a child. When Marilyn Bernardo failed to convince her daughter not to press charges, Paul supplied his father with a reference letter that supported his claim of innocence.

On Valentine's day, Karla gave Paul a special card. 'Honey, I love you with all my heart, now and forever . . . sweet dreams.' In another note, she gushed, 'I will always be totally and undeniably in love with you.' By April 1992, Karla decided to play a bigger role in the couple's sexual exploits by choosing their next victim. She had promised to help Paul round up fifty sex slaves and virgins and was anxious to prove that she was a woman of her word. 'It's Easter soon and do you know what that means? A day off for Karly Curls to spend with her wonderful King. Isn't that great? Miss you. Love you. Karly.'

WORTH DYING FOR

On a grey and damp afternoon in mid-April, Paul and Karla trolled the streets of St Catherine's in their gold Nissan 240SX Sports Coupe in search of a new sex slave toy. Karla pointed to a beautiful 15 year old brunette, Kristen French. She was walking alone. Paul swung the car into a church parking lot. Pretending to be out-of-towners, Karla held out a map, called Kristen over to the car and asked her for directions. When Kristen looked down to study the map, Paul was already out of the driver's seat and behind her with a knife. He threatened to slit Kristen's throat if she screamed. Karla ducked into the back seat of the car while Paul shoved the girl down onto the front bucket seat. Several nearby witnesses saw the scuffle as Karla reached forward, yanked Kristen by the hair, held her down and slammed the passenger door shut. Paul sped away and circled back to the house in Port Dalhousie.

No one noticed as the gold Nissan turned down the driveway at 57 Bayview Street and pulled into the garage. Paul blind-folded Kristen and steered her inside the house through the side door. Once they were inside, Karla proceeded to lock all the

125

doors and shut the blinds. She disconnected the phones but left the answering machine on in case anyone called.

Kristen French was handcuffed when Karla raped her with a glass wine bottle. Using both hands, she rammed the bottle in and out of her anus more than forty times while Paul video-taped the rape and yelled, 'Ram her hard. She called me a bastard.' Paul then videotaped himself raping the girl anally, vaginally and orally as she recited scripted lines and called him, 'the most powerful man in the world', 'the king of kings' and 'master'. Karla pointed the camera at their new hostage and directed the action, shouting, 'Suck him now, Kristen . . . good girl'. To encourage her cooperation, the couple showed Kristen a videotape of Leslie Mahaffy's last tormented hours on Earth.

Paul needed a break and went out for some take-out food. He left Kristen handcuffed and trussed in the closet and gave Karla a rubber mallet to guard her with while he was gone. Kristen begged Karla to let her go but Karla wasn't about to risk her own life to save a stranger's life. Kristen had seen their faces, their house, their car and their dog. Her hours were numbered.

When Paul got back, the trio ate take-out food and watched television. Programming was interrupted by a special news bulletin and a plea from Kristen's dad for his daughter's life. The broadcast upset Kristen so much that Paul popped the movie *Criminal Law* into the VCR. It was his favorite.

After two days of violent rape, terror and degradation involving urination, defecation, sodomy, fellatio and cunnilingus, Karla reminded Paul that her parents were hosting an Easter Sunday dinner. It was time to get rid of the girl. Keeping her any longer was too risky. Paul wanted to make a pornographic movie with her first but Kristen rebelled. 'Some things are worth dying for,' she said, defiantly. 'I don't know how your wife can stand you!'

On Saturday evening, 18 April 1992, Paul went out to rent a video and pick up more fast food. He left Kristen on the floor of the master bedroom with a black electrical cord around her neck that was attached to the handcuffs and restraints binding her feet and hands. When he got back, Kristen was dead on the floor – according to Paul's version of events. While he was out, Kristen had asked Karla if she could go to the washroom and tried to escape. Karla beat her with the rubber mallet causing her to strangle on the neck cord. Karla had a different version of events. She witnessed Paul strangle the girl to death with a black piece of electrical cord on Easter morning.

Karla's mother, Dorothy Homolka, taught her daughters by example. She taught them that it's a wife's duty to clean up after her husband. Like a dutiful wife, Karla cleaned up after Paul. She cleaned out the clogged drains of skin, blood and bone fragments after he sawed up Leslie Mahaffy's body. She douched out his sperm from Kristen French's body and shaved her head so that the police wouldn't be able to trace the carpet fibers.

Paul and Karla drove to a secluded area and dumped Kristen's naked, hairless corpse into a ditch. As they drove away, Paul concluded that what he needed was a house with a specially designed sex-slave dungeon.

The Homolkas greeted their smiling daughter and son-in-law with warm hugs as they arrived at the house for Easter dinner. The famished couple looked as though they'd spent the morning at the local fitness club. Karla gave Paul an Easter card that said, 'To the most wonderful man in the entire world, who means everything to me. All my love, Karly Curls.'

Two weeks later, a scrap metal picker found the naked, battered and blood stained body of Kristen French in a ditch near a garbage dump site.

127

TILL DEATH DO US PART

On 4 May, 1992, Karla received a birthday card from her friend, Debbie. She wrote back to Debbie on 8 May, 'I'm getting pregnant. I can't wait. I'll let you know as things develop'. Karla wrote about 'Spike', her pet iguana, and she wrote about how she and Paul were changing their surname from Bernardo to Teale (like 'Thiel' – the serial killer in the movie *Criminal Law*).

Towards the end of July, Paul's friend, Van Smirnis, came by the house for a visit with a girl named Joann. They watched as Karla's dog, Buddy, chased the pet iguana around the house. When the iguana accidentally bit Paul, he grabbed the terrified creature, slapped it down on the chopping board and beheaded it with a couple of whacks from a kitchen knife. Paul ordered Karla to skin the thing. He flung the skinned iguana on the barbecue and ate it in front of his guests.

Paul's abuse appeared to have no limits. 'You're not to speak to me any more until I say you can,' he told Karla as she accompanied him on a cigarette run across the US border. Whenever she said or did anything he didn't like, he'd say, 'that'll get you ten' or 'this will cost you five' – meaning five or ten punches or beatings. The abuse escalated to include spitting in her food and forcing her to eat his excrement. Karla reasoned that, 'I could do it and get it over with . . . or I could get beaten and then do it.' Paul ordered her to hide in the closet when friends came over because she looked so grotesque.

Karla's internal channel changer stopped working. It was as though the cable company had cut her off and left her with only one channel – the 24 hour nightmare channel. Karla telephoned her father and confided that she wanted to leave Paul. When the Homolkas arrived at the house to pick up their daughter and her belongings, Paul yanked Karla aside and whispered, 'I could show your parents the "Tammy tape". You can't leave me. You can never leave me.' He told her the sex tapes were a one-way ticket to prison and that her family would hate and disown her for raping and killing her own sister. Karla felt trapped. 'I felt like I had to do whatever Paul said because he had this major, horrible thing to hang over my head. I didn't feel like I had a choice and he knew it.' Karla told her parents that she and Paul had patched things up and that she wasn't leaving him after all.

As soon as the Homolkas left, Paul reached for a long handled flashlight and hammered Karla's face and head with it. 'Please whip me, sir, I deserve to be whipped,' Karla begged, using the scripted lines Paul had taught her. He ordered her to strip naked and yelled, 'Down on your knees, bitch . . . Start sucking.' After he was through with her, he shoved her down the basement steps into the damp root cellar and laughed about Leslie Mahaffy's ghost as he flicked off the light, bolted the door and left her there naked. Paul relaxed in front of the TV and watched his favorite home-made souvenir videotapes.

The next time Paul sodomized Karla, he nearly killed her. He yanked so hard on the cord around her neck that she was one gasp away from losing consciousness. Karla feared for her own life.

Karla looked like 'road kill' when she returned to work at the Martindale Animal Clinic on 5 January 1993. Nobody believed her when she said she'd been in a car accident. A co-worker called her mother and said, 'If you want to save your daughter's life, you better hurry.' Dorothy Homolka was horrified at the sight of her daughter who had been punched, kicked, raped, sodomized and choked. The blows to her head and face from the long-handled flashlight had partly dislodged her left eye ball from the socket. She had two racoon-like black eyes, swollen cheeks and lumps and bruises on her arms, legs and forehead. Clumps of her hair were pulled out and her scalp had a spongy texture. Yellowish-brown bruises were also visible from earlier beatings.

Later that day, Karla's mother, father and sister, Lori, pulled up to the house in Port Dalhousie ready to use force, if necessary. 'You're coming with me,' Karla's mother insisted when Karla appeared at the door. Karla resisted. 'I can't leave! You don't understand!' The Homolka's physically dragged her from the house and took her to the hospital emergency. The doctor called it the worst case of wife battering he'd ever seen. After three days in the hospital, Karla explained why she stayed in the abusive relationship for so long. 'I wanted him to love me.'

6

MONSTER ON THE LOOSE

'You're such a vulgar, disgusting sex
maniac. I like that in a man.'
Karla Homolka

Karla Homolka wasn't the only woman to commit serial rape
and murder with a husband accomplice. On the other side of
the Atlantic, another serial sex killer named Rosemary West
was about to be sentenced to life in prison for the sadistic rape,
torture and murder of at least ten young women. Rosemary, a
sexually obsessed bisexual with the face and personality of a pit
bull, raped her victims with a vibrator and forced them to
perform cunnilingus. Many of her victims were found decapi-
tated, dismembered, sexually tortured and buried under her
house in Gloucester, England. Rosemary and her husband, Fred,
fooled their neighbours with a public facade of being a loving
married couple. Their crimes went undetected for twenty years
until a suspicious cop by the name of Hazel Savage arranged for
a search warrant to dig up the Wests' garden at 25 Cromwell
Street. With the discovery of the gruesome carnage, Rosemary
and Fred West joined the ranks of Britain's most notorious sex
killers – right beside Myra Hindley and Ian Brady.

In the 1960s, British serial sex slayer, Myra Hindley, and her
lover, Ian Brady, took children for picnics on the moors. The

children never returned. Their disappearances led to a police investigation and to a three page document in Hindley's car describing how she and Brady had planned the murders. The tabloids called Hindley and Brady the 'Moors Murderers' and labeled them the most brutal, sadistic child sex slayers in twentieth-century Britain. What made this case unique is that it was the first time in British history that a woman had been involved in a serial sex-slaying partnership involving children. The public could not fathom how a woman could willingly participate in such a diabolical crime. Hindley became a female icon of evil.

LITTLE RED RIDING HOODS

Like Britain's Myra Hindley and Rosemary West, America's Charlene Williams was a sexually obsessed killer who teamed up with boyfriend accomplice, Gerald Gallego, and went on a killing spree across Oregon, Nevada and California. Charlene kidnapped female victims at gunpoint, two at a time, and forced the kidnapped girls to have sex with her in the back of a van fitted with a mattress. Eric van Hoffmann, who conducted an in-depth study of the case, reported that 'Charlene liked to bite one of the girls while the other brought her to climax with oral sex, and in one case, bit off the victim's nipple'. All of the victims were killed and either dumped off or buried in shallow graves after being beaten to death with a hammer or shot 'execution style'. Charlene plea bargained a reduced sentence of 16 years in prison in exchange for testifying against Gallego who got the death penalty.

Carol Bundy teamed up with 'Sunset Strip Killer', Douglas Clark, and brought an end to the LAPD manhunt in 1980 when she was apprehended for sawing off a man's head with a boning knife. Veronica Compton joined 'Hillside Strangler' Kenneth Bianchi, and attempted her own copycat strangling. 'Women like us aren't as rare as we thought,' observed Carol Bundy, when she found out Veronica Compton was occupying a neighbouring jail cell. Death row inmate, Judith Ann Neely, rounded up sex slaves for husband, Alvin. She is awaiting execution in Alabama for killing her captives, one of whom she shot and threw over a cliff after injecting her with Drano.

Women who participate in killer partnerships typically pin the blame on their abusive mates. Once caught, they cast themselves as 'Little Red Riding Hoods' and testify against their big bad wolf partners in exchange for a reduced sentence. Typically, Karla Homolka took the witness stand and showed her big wolf what a big mouth she had.

THE BIG BAD WOLF

Paul Kenneth Bernardo was arrested and charged on 6 January, 1993 with 'assault with a weapon' after hammering his wife's face with a long handled steel flashlight. Karla told the police that Paul assaulted her at least once every day since July of 1992.

Since Paul had no previous record, he was released on his own recognizance. Feeling alone, abandoned and suicidal, the 'King of Kings' returned to their house in Port Dalhousie and proceeded to drink, pop pills, howl and sob. On 10 January 1993, five days after Karla left him, he recorded a goodbye-cruel-world suicide monologue into his micro cassette recorder. Using his nice-guy voice and some background music, he sniffled and snuffled into a microphone about his undying love for his 'Karly Curls', for his 'babes,' for his little 'snuggle bunny'. 'I don't know if I ever told you this, but I love you, too, Kar. You were my rock, you know. My security. My stability.'

Karla's dog, Buddy, knew better than to howl as Paul's monologue dragged on 'I need you, Kar. I love you, my princess, my queen, my everything . . . guess what, pal? I cry a lot . . . I wanted to be greater than anything that ever was and when I didn't reach it, I got frustrated and angry . . . and I took it out on you – the person I love the most! Don't hate me for that . . . just please don't hate me for my mom's genetics . . . We were the best, man. The envy of everybody . . . United we stand together. I'm going to fall for us . . . My life's over. I've got nothing. I'm less than zero . . . at times it wasn't me. I don't know what it was, but it wasn't me . . . I was born a bastard and I'll die a bastard . . . When you know you've lost it all and there is no one to turn to, death's welcome mat is the only place you can go. You know I love you, man . . . I tried to be the best that there ever was, maybe because I needed love . . . '

Six days after his suicide tape, Paul was still alive and kicking. He decided to make another long winded recording. 'I wanted to love you but I was hurt. No one understood me. Bad guys like me gotta go. Born a bastard. Died the bastard. I've always been a bastard, a very bad bastard, very bad person. You're the best . . . I've cried a million tears, Kar. I don't know how to stop . . . I really wasn't that bad a guy . . . I just tried too hard. I tried to be too macho. Too domineering. I thought those were the qualities that were important to be successful. But I forgot a lot of the qualities like the qualities you have. I forgot how to cherish and love . . . I'm just an asshole . . . I have an undying love for you and a hatred towards myself . . . You were my support system . . . we deserve to be together . . . the best fucking couple in the world . . . The grim reaper's coming. I'm afraid, Kar. I'm so afraid. He's outside my door. He's coming for me.'

A HIDEOUT

Karla was worried. After missing three menstrual periods, she was worried that she might be pregnant. Paul once told her that 'if he'd ever had a girl, he'd have had sex with her. Karla was also worried about Buddy. 'Paul better not be abusing him or there will be hell to pay,' she warned. Karla's aunt and uncle from Brampton, Ontario, kindly offered Karla their home as a safe haven. It was only an hour's drive from St Catherine's. Karla accepted their invitation and spent her time collecting her thoughts and itemizing Paul's trespasses – his mind manipulation, his threats, the ulcers he'd caused. 'He made me sleep in the root cellar; threw knives at me; said he would kill me and make it look like an accident; couldn't go to bed until he said I could . . . I was always terrified when I was with him.' Karla detailed how Paul had punched, kicked and battered her for no reason at all and even admitted that he had no conscience, no remorse, no regrets.

MEANWHILE . . .

Without Karla, Paul desperately needed a plan. He needed to figure out a way of capturing young female prey without Karla's help. In a flash of brilliance, the answer came to him. He would become a rap singer, a white man's version of 'MC Hammer'. The girls would be tearing at his clothes, falling at his feet, begging to do whatever he wanted them to do. He'd need a change of image, his own sound studio and some recording equipment.

Paul got his ears pierced and styled his blond locks into ringlets. He installed a synthesizer and other equipment in a sound-proofed bedroom, then proceeded to drink, pop pills and compose his rap album. When Karla discovered that Paul had been getting cash advances on all her credit cards, she hired a divorce lawyer and cut Paul off financially. With no money to finance his album, Paul tried luring Karla back home. He decided to resort to more extreme measures when his best efforts failed to get results.

Paul drove over to the Shaver Medical Clinic where Karla's mother, Dorothy, worked. He pulled into the parking lot and waited. As soon as he spotted Dorothy exiting from the building, he confronted her face to face. Dorothy froze in her tracks. 'Do you really think Tammy's death was an accident?' he asked, venomously. 'Do you really think your daughter didn't have anything to do with her death?' Dorothy ducked into her car and sped away.

FINDING A GOOD EXCUSE

Karla was interviewed by a couple of detectives who informed her that her husband was a suspect in a series of sexual assaults. Nothing about Paul surprised her, she said innocently, as she described Paul's threats and beatings and explained that she only married him because she had no other choice. When the police asked her for her fingerprints, Karla was knocked off-guard. None of it was her fault, she stammered defensively. Paul forced her to do what she did.

After the police left, Karla confessed to her aunt and uncle that she knew for a fact that Paul was the Scarborough rapist and that he had killed Leslie Mahaffy and Kristen French. She told them Paul threatened to kill her family and even went to her parents' house one night and broke a window to prove he wasn't bluffing. He said, 'I could've killed your whole family. I was that close.' The Segers advised Karla to get a lawyer immediately. Karla picked up the phone and got criminal lawyer George Walker on the line. He agreed to meet with her.

136

Looking cool and aloof, Karla gave Walker a blow-by-blow description of the sadism, the videotaped pornography and the grisly sex slayings. Walker needed to size up the pretty, battered, pleading young woman sitting across from him. 'Is she the hapless victim of a diabolical Svengali?' he asked himself. To defend her, he'd need to come up with a hell of a good defense strategy. PMS and amnesia had been used successfully as a defense in other cases. Lorena Bobbitt got off with the Battered Wife Syndrome and the Post Traumatic Stress double whammy – but Karla didn't fit the Battered Wife Syndrome profile. Women who suffer from that syndrome strike out at their abusers. Instead of striking out at Paul, Karla participated in the kidnapping and confinement of teenage girls, sexually assaulted them and videotaped the assaults, served her younger sister to her rapist fiancé like Christmas cake. Walker chose to go with the compliant accomplice defense and he'd blame the whole thing on Paul. Karla warned Walker that she wouldn't testify against Paul without blanket immunity.

George Walker contacted the police. He informed them that Paul Bernardo had killed Leslie Mahaffy and Kristen French and that he had also videotaped the sexual assaults and forced his client to participate. In a follow-up meeting with his client, Walker told Karla that a prison sentence was unavoidable and that blanket immunity was totally out of the question. The most she could ever hope for would be a reduced sentence in exchange for testifying against Paul.

X-RATED LIBRARY

Paul's earlier DNA tests that had been mysteriously misplaced for two years suddenly showed up at the sexual assault squad office. Armed with a 900-page document and a search warrant, the police ransacked the house of horrors in Port Dalhousie on 17 February 1993. They arrested and handcuffed a non-combative Paul Bernardo at gun point for the murders of Leslie Mahaffy and Kristen French and for 53 other offenses dating back to 1983. The criminal charges included nine counts of sexual assault with a weapon, aggravated sexual assault, wounding, sodomy, assault with a deadly weapon, buggery, kidnapping, five counts of anal intercourse, forcible confinement, indignity to a human body and two murders. Paul pleaded not guilty to all of the charges. That same year, Paul's father, Ken Bernardo, who had pleaded not guilty to a charge of sexual assault, was sentenced to nine months in jail and three years probation for indecently assaulting a nine-year-old girl.

A search of the Port Dalhousie house uncovered triple 'X' collections of pornographic books and videotapes. The movie, *American Psycho* was Paul's Bible. Patrick Bateman, who had the same initials as Paul, was his rapist hero. Paul dressed just like his hero in yuppie designer clothes and he shared Bateman's sadistic hatred of women. He even described women using the same misogynist slurs that Bateman used like 'fucking whore' and 'bitch' and believed that 'women who don't submit and comply should be cut up'. Paul's favorite story books included *Devil Child* and books featuring descriptions of rats being inserted into women's vaginas and intercourse with woman's severed heads. Son of Sam, Ted Bundy, and Hillside Strangler books joined Paul's collection of role model reading material. His video collection specialized in psychopathic killers, satanism and necrophilia and contained scenes of women being slaughtered with power drills, scissors, chainsaws and knives. Karla starred in many of the home-made sex tapes including one with close-ups of her performing oral sex on a comatose girl.

SUGAR SHACK

Karla felt like a prisoner. Several nosy reporters were camped on her aunt and uncle's doorstep hoping for a scoop. To throw them off, Karla disguised herself in a black wig, sunglasses, hat, halter top and tight blue jeans before venturing over to the local shopping mall. On 5 February, she persuaded her aunt to take her out on the town for a change of scenery. They drove to the Sugar Shack bar and ordered a couple of drinks. Like a kid in a candy store, Karla scanned the smoke-filled room and checked out all the available men. She danced. She drank. And she had sex with a complete stranger.

SORRY FOLKS

Karla returned home to St Catherine's to face manslaughter charges. She was admitted to the psychiatric ward of Northwestern General Hospital for seven weeks of observation and testing while her attorney, the police and prosecutors negotiated a plea-bargain deal. From the hospital, she wrote a damage control letter to her family.

Dear Mom, Dad and Lori,

This is the hardest letter I've ever had to write and you'll probably all hate me once you've read it. I've kept this to myself for so long and I just can't lie to you any more. Both Paul and I are responsible for Tammy's death. Paul was 'in love' with her and wanted to have sex with her. He wanted me to help him. He wanted me to get sleeping pills from work to drug her with. He threatened me and physically and emotionally abused me when I refused. No words I can say can make you understand what he put me through. So stupidly I agreed to do as he said. But something – maybe the combination of the drugs and the food she ate that

139

night – caused her to vomit. I tried so hard to save her. I am so sorry. But no words I can say can bring her back. I have thought many times of killing myself, but I couldn't put you through the pain of losing another daughter and sister again. I don't blame you all if you hate me. I hate myself. I live with the pain of knowing I unintentionally killed my baby sister every day. I think that's the real reason I put up with Paul's abusive behaviour – I felt I deserved it for allowing him to drug and rape my beautiful baby sister. I loved her so much and never wanted to do anything to hurt my 'Tamsikins', please believe me. I would gladly give my life for hers. Nothing I can do or say can bring her back. I don't expect you to ever forgive me, for I will never forgive myself.

Karla, XOXO

On behalf of the Homolka family, Karla's only remaining sister, Lori, wrote back to Karla.

Dear Karla,

We all seem to think that you feel we are going to abandon you and not love you any more because of what has happened. Please don't ever think that way. We're your family, Kar, and we love you uncon- ditionally. What has happened to you is in no way your fault, you did what you had to do to survive and we are so glad for that. You are such an incredibly strong person which I have always admired.

Your pissy little sissy,
Lori

MAD OR BAD?

A team of mental health experts couldn't figure out if Karla was pathologically 'mad' or psychopathically 'bad'. The psychiatrists had conflicting interpretations of Karla's test results. Dr Allan Long observed that people like Karla 'feel socially inadequate, alienated, confused and lack trust in others. They may be confused and distractible and are frequently diagnosed as schizophrenic.' Dr Long described Karla as 'a leader and somewhat bossy' and concluded from the Rorschach and TAT tests that rather than being 'depressed, withdrawn and remorseful', Karla was 'immature, moody, shallow, rigid, hostile'. Noting that she was 'preoccupied with themes of violence and victimization', he did not consider her anxiety and depression to be the effects of Battered Woman's Syndrome or Post-Traumatic Stress Syndrome but rather the result of a fear of being prosecuted and jailed.

Dr Pollack concluded from Karla's MMPI personality test results that Karla saw herself as 'conventional, moralistic' and 'does what is right'. She is the type of person who craves attention and affection, is easily slighted and typically forms shallow and exploitive relationships with little concern for anyone but herself. She saw herself as confident and socially adept but others saw her as narcissistic and egocentric. Karla's personality type is often diagnosed with 'histrionic, obsessive-compulsive and/or passive-aggressive features' – traits of a psychopath.

Dr Peter Jaffe, an abuse specialist, stated that Karla was 'groomed by Mr Bernardo to become involved in increasingly bizarre and dangerous behaviour that was harmful to herself and others'. Jaffe believed Karla was very vulnerable prior to meeting Paul Bernardo. She had written a suicide note in junior high school and showed it to a friend. In the note, she said, 'I don't like me. I am no longer the person I used to be. I am different . . . I

141

have reached the end. I have nobody to turn to. I am thinking and nothing makes sense. I end up with one thought. Suicide. This is the one thought that makes sense. The only one. It is hard to take a life, yet so easy . . . I wish I could turn back time to my simple, yet happy childhood. I was so carefree. So happy. I had no problems. I am caught up in this world. A nightmare . . . ' In Dr Jaffe's opinion, Karla's vulnerability was accentuated by the difference in power and status based on Paul's age, life experience, education and physical size advantage. She 'exhibits all the signs and symptoms of a young woman who has been severely traumatized by an abusive relationship . . . she fits all the criteria for the Battered Women's Syndrome.'

The nagging question that remained was, 'how could Karla be battered and brain-washed and also be strong willed with a superior range of intelligence in the top two per cent of the population?' With the exception of Dr Jaffe's conclusions, Karla was, according to the diagnostic consensus, a severely disturbed borderline personality, a histrionic, a psychopath.

BRAIN WASHED?

Other behavioural-science experts believed that Karla was literally 'captivated' by Paul Bernardo and that her sense of self and self-worth were slowly and insidiously eroded by him until she became an instrument of his will and even abandoned her own opinions. Brainwashing can sometimes occur when a person is isolated, psychologically tormented and deprived of sleep. Brainwashed prisoners in Nazi concentration camps reportedly kissed the boots of their captors who they perceived as having supreme authority and power over them. Their very survival depended on complying to their captor's demands at any and all costs. Paul Bernardo was thought to have intentionally isolated, tormented, abused and consequently brainwashed Karla Homolka into participating in the sexual assaults and murders.

HYBRISTOPHILIAC?

Psychiatric literature identifies a disorder called Hybristophilia – 'the phenomenon of a woman who is sexually turned on only by a partner with a sexual history of rape and pillage'. Hybristophiliacs taunt and provoke their partners to commit sadistic, inhumane acts and, by so doing, vicariously live out their own perverse fantasies. Martha Beck, a rotund nurse, persuaded Raymond Fernandez to murder the women he was swindling. 'It seems to have been the partnership with Martha that turned him into "America's most hated killer"', noted Wilson and Seaman in their book, *Serial Killers*. Charlene Williams, was also suspected of turning her serial sex killer partner, Gerald Gallego, into her manipulated victim. Was Karla Homolka an hybristophiliac who encouraged, taunted, provoked, lured and transformed Paul Bernardo into a serial murderer as well as a serial rapist?

Some observers saw Karla Homolka and Paul Bernardo as 'an evil entity greater than the sum of its parts'. SPD or 'Shared Psychotic Disorder' occurs when a charismatic lover gradually infuses their more suggestible partner with paranoid delusions and fantasies resulting in shared distortions of reality and a shared madness. The charismatic partner in the union is, more often than not, the woman.

VACUOUS?

Dr Angus McDonald observed that Karla's 'relatively aggressive presentation at times does not seem consistent with the view of her as a fearful, terribly dominated individual lacking the spine

143

to stand up for herself.' McDonald claimed that Karla's behaviour 'cannot be explained solely on the basis of intimidation and abuse'. He noted that there was a moral vacuity to her. 'Karla Homolka remains something of a diagnostic mystery', reported McDonald.

DIAGNOSTIC MYSTERY?

Karla Homolka was no diagnostic mystery to author Patricia Pearson. She did it all for image, concluded Pearson after researching, studying and analyzing the case. By blackening both her eyes, Paul, who was Karla's 'fantasy, trophy and obsession', crossed the one boundary that Karla held dear – the image boundary. 'For the image of the perfect love, she had allowed women to die.' By blackening both her eyes, Paul shattered Karla's world of pretend. She could no longer look in the mirror and pretend to be 'the envy of everybody'. That was the one critical difference between them, claims Pearson. 'Homolka needed approval. Bernardo did not. He came to understand that if he stayed by her side playing the excellent gentleman in public, he could foray ever deeper into private perversion without risk of exposure. For exposure was his wife's idea of hell.'

Karla turned the Dalhousie house upside down looking for the incriminating videotapes but came up empty. Like a quick-change artist, she shed her attention-getting 'Barbie' image for an even-more-attention-getting 'Battered Wife' image. Her attentive family took her home with them. Rape, murder and battery couldn't get Karla to walk out on Paul. 'Breaking her Barbie doll face' is all it took.

JAYWALKING

Tammy Lynn Homolka's body was exhumed and the investigation into her death reopened. Karla's lawyer struck a deal in top-secret negotiations with police and prosecutors. Since Karla Homolka was coerced by Paul Bernardo and had no choice, she would be completely exonerated in the death of her sister and would escape all sexual assault charges. In exchange for a mandatory 12 year sentence for manslaughter, Karla agreed to appear in court as the abused compliant victim of a sexual sadist.

When he found out about Karla's deal with prosecutors, Paul took a tantrum and cursed, 'Fucking system! . . . bitch is sicker 'n me and she's gonna get off!' This self-professed little 'cocksucker-cunt-slut' who joined him on a kidnapping, rape and killing spree was going to put him away for life and all she gets is jaywalking?

THEY HATE THEIR MOMS

Roy Hazelwood, who studied serial-rapist killers and their girlfriends for seventeen years, pioneered the bizarre phenomenon known as 'compliant victims'. His research of compliant women is the most extensive in the field. As a behavioural science expert and criminal profiler with the FBI, Hazelwood assisted in thousands of homicide and rape cases. 'To understand women like Karla Homolka, you must first understand the man who controls them'. Serial sex-killers like Paul Bernardo often grow up in households with weak or absent father figures. Many were illegitimate, unwanted and subjected to severe childhood sexual, physical and emotional abuse. Their efforts to show love as children were met with brutality and punishment. To escape the brutality, they retreated into a private world of obsessive and grotesque fantasy which became stored as toxic rage towards all of humanity. Instead of equating sex with love, serial sex-killers equate sex with aggression, domination and murderous rage.

'They hate their moms. We hear that repeatedly,' says Hazelwood. Like two-year-olds in adult bodies, they pick things up only to break and destroy them – and people are no exception. Although their libido may be strong, it is power, anger and the need to control, not sex, that motivates them. Their desire to get back at somebody, to make others suffer and pay for their misery, consumes them so that they can only experience pleasure by causing pain. Sex is their weapon of choice. Power is their motive. Love is something they can only fake through an intellectual understanding of it. Overwhelmed with despair and self-loathing, serial rapists and killers experience temporary relief during their crimes by creating a sense of personal control. Some sexual psychopaths collect souvenir videos of their crimes the way other people collect vacation videos. They record the screams and pain of their victims so that they can relive the morbid moments over and over again. One sexual sadist who planned to build a dungeon equipped with an incinerator, described his need 'to become her god, to do with her as one pleases, to humiliate her, to enslave her, since there is no greater power over another person than that of inflicting pain on her, to force her to undergo suffering without her being able to defend herself. The pleasure of complete domination over another person is the very essence of the sadistic drive.' The sexual psychopath's own death wish is often the catalyst responsible for their demise as they carelessly engineer their own capture and death by execution or suicide.

COMPLIANT ACCOMPLICES

What makes serial sex-killers so frightening is their friendly facade and their capacity to commit gruesome, violent acts. They are not raving lunatics, the devil incarnate or hideous-looking Hollywood villains. Most are witty, charming, intelligent, appealing, convincingly ordinary and capable of conning female partners – which enables them to elude detection for so long.

Hazelwood interviewed fifteen women who had formed partnerships with sexual sadists and participated in serial rapes and killings. All fifteen came from middle to upper-class backgrounds with average or better intelligence and good jobs. All had a history of low self-esteem, lacked confidence and described the same kinds of emotional, physical and sexual abuse. All, except one, became addicted to alcohol and drugs and only one had previous sado-masochistic experiences. The women were typically conned by their abusers who told them childhood stories about being abused and unloved. Which aroused the women's maternal instincts and a need to prove that not all women are alike. The relationship began as a caring one, then threats of abandonment became a manipulative way of getting the woman to participate in his games that started with capture, struggle and rape scenarios and scripted statements like, 'Please don't kill me, master.'

Four of the 15 women helped in the murders and one helped kill ten women. All 15 suffered regular beatings and were held captive, 14 submitted to bondage, 14 were recorded with photos or videos of their sex acts, 14 were verbally abused, 12 were verbally scripted, ten were bitten, eight were whipped, six were subjected to ligature strangulation during sex. All 15 women plea bargained a prison term of five to 15 years in exchange for testifying against their partners.

A SEX KILLER'S FIVE STEP FORMULA

According to Roy Hazelwood, the sex killer follows a basic five step formula in the ultimate takeover of his female partners-in-crime:

STEP ONE: He finds a naive, passive vulnerable woman who is depressed about herself and easy to manipulate and therefore easy to degrade and humiliate.

STEP TWO: He charms her into falling in love with him by acting considerate, unselfish, attentive, daring, romantic and generous, then he seduces and manipulates her into satisfying him.

STEP THREE: Once her affection is firmly established, he gradually introduces her to a kinky smorgasbord of bondage, fellatio, dildos, sodomy, photographed and videotaped sex. He teaches her to protect their 'special relationship' and to smile for the camera (like so many sexually abused children smile for family photographs and protect their abuser).

STEP FOUR: He gives positive reinforcement and affection for submissive behaviour that allows him to dominate, control and perform sadistic acts on her. He punishes her with negative reinforcement and threats of abandonment for resistance and bad behaviour until what was infrequent and abnormal becomes frequent and normal.

STEP FIVE: He isolates her from her friends by appearing possessive and jealous at first. He criticizes her mercilessly for independent activities until her world becomes progressively more confined and her emotional dependency so intense that she is transformed into an obedient object of his psychological and physical punishment.

'Having met, seduced and transformed a nice woman into a sexually compliant, totally dependent individual, the sadist has validated his theory of women,' says Hazelwood. 'The woman is now a subservient, inferior being who had allowed herself to be recreated sexually and has participated in sexual acts that no decent woman would engage in thereby confirming she is a "bitch" deserving of punishment.' Karla Homolka confirmed and proved true all of Paul Bernardo's twisted beliefs about women. She licked, sucked and obeyed on cue. She called him 'master' and 'king of kings' and she called herself 'slut', 'whore', 'cocksucker' and 'ass licker' all in the right order. Karla Homolka became everything Paul loved to hate. Public reaction to compliant women accomplices is outrage, says Hazelwood, because the average person cannot understand how anyone could act the way these women did or accept the conditions that lead them to that point. When a compliant woman accomplice talks about the criminal offense, there is an emotional deadness to her speech. 'She has been conditioned not to register any emotion or feelings,' explains Hazelwood who rejects any suggestions that these women are 'evil'.

FOOLING THE EXPERTS

Roy Hazelwood's compliant accomplice theory suggests that women with poor self-esteem can be recreated into obedient, murderous sex slaves in five easy steps and are as bubble-brained and shapeable as a wad of chewing gum. To believe Hazelwood's theory is to believe that 'dominant' males can con 'helpless' females into participating in insane criminal behaviour by taking over their will. Patricia Pearson criticizes the FBI paradigm as 'demeaning to an entire sex'. It suggests that any woman would have behaved like Homolka in her circumstances and assumes

149

that 'a woman's stake in deviant behaviour can never be self interest', since she is 'incapable of intending any real harm'.

In spite of the fact that seventeen per cent of serial killers in the United States are women and in spite of the statistical evidence of widespread female violence towards children, newborns, spouses and the elderly, our culture continues to stubbornly deny women's innate capacity for physical and sexual aggression, particularly if the women are heterosexual, cute and feminine.

'Paul did it'. 'Paul made me do it', repeated Karla Homolka as she peddled her claim of innocence to the legal, medical and mental health professionals. Her only sin, she proclaimed was 'to pick the wrong man for a husband'. By stroking male prejudice about women's non-aggressive, sexually passive nature, Karla Homolka convinced her judicial male entourage that her violent behaviour was not deliberate and that she never intended any harm. Admitting that women are responsible for their crimes of violence by intending to cause harm is tantamount to admitting that women are threatening and a force to be reckoned with.

WHO CONTROLLED WHO?

How could an out-of-control sexual predator like Paul Bernardo control an intelligent, manipulative woman like Karla Homolka when he couldn't even control himself? Was Karla Homolka, with her superior range of intelligence and strong-willed personality, putty in the hands of a sexual predator, or was Paul Bernardo putty in the hands of a Lady Macbeth who encouraged, taunted and provoked his crimes? When Karla first met Paul Bernardo, she found him challenging. 'With other guys, I could always do what I wanted and that was boring . . .

In my previous relationships, I was in total control.' Karla's flurry of encouraging letters to Paul expressed how 'turned on' she was by his perversions -'don't rip off my clothes and ravish me like a beast for a solid hour . . . do it all night long.' Another note said, 'roses are red, violets are blue. There's nothing more fun than a pervert like you' and in another, 'you're such a vulgar, disgusting sex maniac. I like that in a man.' On their first date, Karla handcuffed her hands behind her back, got down on her knees and told him to lift up her skirt. When Paul asked her how she'd feel if he told her he was a rapist, she answered, 'Cool'. Karla introduced Paul to *Criminal Law*, a 'slasher-maniac' movie about a sadistic serial rapist called 'Thiel', who not only rapes his victims but murders them and destroys the evidence. Karla was a 'Thiel' fan who initiated Paul Bernardo into her Thiel fan club. She groomed him to become so much like her rape-movie idol that he even changed his name to Teale (Thiel). To conclude that the smut collection found by police at the Port Dalhousie house was Paul's collection is an erroneous assumption. The collection was co-owned by Paul and Karla who watched replays of their sexual assaults including the videotapes which Karla herself had directed and shot. Together, they watched, relived and got high on their souvenir moments as Karla anally raped Kristen French with a wine bottle, performed oral sex on a comatose girl, donned her dead sister's underwear and suggested to Paul that they abduct fifty more virgins.

Contrary to popular belief, it was Karla Homolka who controlled Paul Bernardo. She controlled him by supplying him with virgins and by satisfying his perverse sexual fantasies. She controlled him by planning the kidnapping of Kristen French and the rape of her own sister. Karla chose the victim, supervised the rapes, directed the videos, guarded the hostages, decided the time of their execution, disposed of their bodies and masterminded the cover-ups. Like a drug pusher supplying drugs to an addict, Karla supplied Paul's sexual addictions. He needed her with a child-like dependency that he revealed in his 'goodbye-cruel-world' suicide tape to his 'Snuggle Bunny' – 'You were my rock, you know. My security. My stability . . . You were my support system . . . I'm going to fall for us . . . ', he boo-hooed after Karla abandoned him.

GETTING AWAY WITH MURDER

Paul Bernardo was a serial rapist, a sadist and a sexual pervert but was he a murderer? Prior to meeting Karla Homolka, his criminal profile as the Scarborough Rapist was that of a serial rapist, not a serial killer. Paul's ultimate fantasy was to own a 'virgin farm' populated with obedient virgin sex slaves who would cater to his every need and call him 'Master'. Prior to meeting Karla, Paul released all of the women he raped. His thrill was the hunt, the capture and the degradation of women, not the kill. From the time Paul and Karla abducted Leslie Mahaffy and Kristen French to the time of their death, Bernardo took the precaution of blindfolding the girls. He blindfolded them for one reason – because he intended to let them go just as he'd always done in the past. Bernardo was an angry child inside a man's body. Like a child, he viewed his captives as toys and playthings that he wanted to keep. Karla viewed them as rivals that she wanted to get rid of. They were her 'doggie treats' for her 'mad dog husband'.

After killing her own sister-rival, Karla had few reservations about killing total strangers who could potentially identify her and Bernardo and send them to prison for the rest of their unnatural lives. She had administered the fatal overdose of

152

animal anaesthetic that caused Tammy Homolka to vomit and choke to death. She had disposed of the drugs and covered up the incriminating evidence while Paul frantically tried to revive Tammy with mouth-to-mouth resuscitation. Paul desperately wanted to save the 15-year-old girl he'd just raped because somewhere in the dark recesses of his twisted mind, he believed he was in love with her.

Paul Bernardo's lawyer, John Rosen, painted Karla Homolka as someone who would sacrifice sister, iguana, schoolgirls and as many hymens as it took to keep her man from leaving her. Rosen accused Homolka of murdering Leslie Mahaffy by suffocation and of killing Kristen French by beating her with a rubber mallet causing the girl to strangle on the cord noosed around her neck. The superficial marks and chafing on Kristen's neck were inconsistent with Karla's testimony that Paul strangled her for seven minutes. Chief forensic pathologist, Dr David King, who performed autopsies on Leslie Mahaffy and Tammy Homolka and who reviewed the autopsy report on Kristen French, stated, 'I do not think Kristen French died from ligature strangulation and I certainly don't think she died from having an electrical cord tied around her neck for seven minutes. There's no way'. King confirmed that the bruises on Kristen's face were inflicted by blows from a blunt object, possibly a rubber mallet. He also confirmed that there were knee-size imprints on the backs of both girls. Rosen charged that Homolka kneeled on the backs of both girls and that she suffocated Leslie Mahaffy by pressing her face into a pillow while she was in a drugged stupor and while Paul was out on an errand.

When Homolka's deal with prosecutors made headlines, the public was lynch-mob irate. In exchange for testifying against Paul Bernardo, Karla Homolka would get a 12-year sentence and be eligible for parole in just four years. The woman who had drugged, raped, videotaped and murdered her own sister and who had kidnapped, drugged, tortured, raped, video-taped and murdered Leslie Mahaffy and Kristen French and who had also drugged, raped and videotaped Jane Doe, could be back on the street by 1998 and eligible to go home on unescorted weekend day passes even sooner. Hundreds of thousands of outraged citizens protested, signed petitions and lobbied politicians to have the sentence overturned. The deal-makers defended their decision – a deal is a deal.

EXCERPTS FROM THE TRIAL

They lined up four abreast outside the courthouse entrance. The streets were jammed with zealous reporters, TV crews and people waving banners. To insure that Paul Bernardo got a fair trial, a publication ban was ordered to muzzle the press.

Karla came to court prepared. She studied up on Lenore Walker's Battered Woman Syndrome and learned everything she needed to know about the role of battered women and their psychological profiles. On 19 June 1995, wearing a navy blue dress, blond hair tied in a ponytail, Karla confidently stepped up onto the witness stand to pin the blame on Paul Bernardo in nine days of testimony and seven days of cross examination.

Looking as innocent as a choirboy, Paul sat quietly in his orange prison overalls observing his wife from the defendants box. Like a seasoned veteran, his lawyer, John Rosen, strolled into the legal arena, took aim at Karla Homolka and started firing.

ROSEN: You were madly, passionately desperate for this man over here to be part of your life.

154

KARLA: Yes, I was passionately in love with him and yes, I wanted him to be part of my life, and I have never denied that.

ROSEN: Your position, as I understand it, is that whatever you did, whatever involvement you had in these offenses is because you were brutalized, terrorized, and controlled by your husband, Paul Bernardo?

Rosen draws the jury's attention to an intimate card that Karla wrote to Paul cordially inviting him to 'fuck the shit out of me' and another one, 'You're a vulgar, disgusting sex maniac. I like that in a man.' Rosen challenged Karla's excuses for staying in the relationship. He reminded her that she had numerous opportunities to find the incriminating Tammy/French/Mahaffy videotapes and destroy them and that Paul had more to lose by exposing the tapes than she did. Her excuse that she feared Paul would expose her to her family was total nonsense, contended Rosen, who charged that Karla didn't fear or hate Bernardo. She stayed with him because she was obsessed with him.

ROSEN: You're the one who could have said 'no' at any time, but you kept saying 'yes' and 'yes'.

KARLA: I did not want my parents to know that anything was wrong in my relationship. A lot of women go through this. It is not unusual for a woman to go through this type of relationship and still think they love them.

ROSEN: You're living with someone you hate and who is talking about abducting a girl right off the street and yet you don't rush into the police station and say, 'I'm living with a maniac and you've got to stop him before somebody else gets hurt?'

KARLA: No.

Karla sat in the witness box as plastic and as unemotional as a store mannequin while Rosen expressed his disgust for a woman who could serve up her own sister as a Christmas present in a deadly game of sexual molestation.

ROSEN: You thought: If my sister thinks she can play with fire and not get burned, I'll show her!

KARLA: You are dead wrong.

ROSEN: We're talking about your little sister. You were her elder sister. Your parents trusted you to look after her, didn't they?

KARLA: I didn't believe she was in jeopardy.

ROSEN: (exploding) Do you not understand that what was being planned and discussed was the rape of your little sister while she was unconscious in your parents' and your home?

KARLA: Yes, I understand that. I was absolutely terrified and didn't feel I had a choice. Now I know I had a choice . . . I have to live with this every day of my life.

ROSEN: What you have to live with is that you participated because you were into kinky sex the same as he was.

KARLA: That's a lie.

156

Karla's explanation for giving in to Paul's Christmas request for her sister's virginity was that 'he kept bugging me'. She explained that she numbed out through it all and got numb and number as the abuse continued.

> KARLA: When Tammy first died I felt numb. Then when Leslie was kidnapped I felt number and when Kristen was in the house I felt even number.

'Numb and Number' might be a good title for a Hollywood movie but it makes a helluva lousy excuse for rape and murder. After sixteen days on the witness stand, Karla became progressively more combatant and cocky, often responding to Rosen's attacks with, 'That's a lie' and 'That's absolutely ridiculous'.

The jury sat through graphic slow-motion scenes from the videotaped atrocities showing the naked girls tearfully pleading for mercy as the 'bruiseless' Karla Homolka forced sadistic sex acts on them in concert with Paul. Together with the girls' agonizing screams, the jury heard Karla's voice shouting directions at the victims while Paul raped them.

Crown Attorney Ray Houlahan questioned Karla about a scene in one of the home-made sex tapes.

> HOULAHAN: And what are you doing there, Ms Homolka?
>
> KARLA: Well, I'm performing cunnilingus on her, and then I'm inserting a wine bottle in her anus.

After completing her testimony, Karla briefly glanced across the courtroom at her 'Big Bad Businessman' sitting in the prisoner's box. He mouthed the words, 'Fuck you.' Karla's lips parted into a vague smile that seemed to say, 'Goodbye Snuffles'.

As a result of Karla's damning testimony, Paul Kenneth Bernardo was found guilty on all nine counts of murder, rape and kidnapping on 1 September 1995. He was sentenced to life in prison with no parole for 25 years and warehoused in a special, windowless plexiglass isolation cell at the Kingston Penitentiary.

'A wimp and a cry baby easily reduced to tears and silence'. That's how inmates described the new resident, Paul Bernardo, who passes the time in his isolation cell writing rap songs. His lyrics attempt to disguise his fears and his failed macho complex by talking tough to little girls. 'I'm the solo creep, I make the girls weep, committing my crimes while others sleep . . . I've got no remorse and I've got no shame.' 'You think I'm innocent? . . . I'm packing a lot of deadliness, so, come at me, come at me, I got a fucking nice face, I look like a pretty boy, why don't you come at me, man? Take your best shot. See what happens to you, pal. You're outta here, man. You come at me with your beer belly and you think you're really tough. I come back, looking like I'm 13 years old. I'll kick your ass. I'll kill your parents. Then I'll shoot your girlfriend. And fuck your wife. That's me, deadly innocence.'

CLUB FED

Karla Homolka received a 12-year sentence in a plea deal to testify against her husband, Paul Bernardo. Prosecutors agreed to the deal before they were aware of videotapes of the crimes which showed Homolka as a willing, eager participant. 'There's been worse and there will be worse crimes,' said her father, Karel Homolka, who visited his daughter at Kingston, Ontario's prison for women where she was initially incarcerated.

Separated from the main prison population, Karla gave her prison cell a make-over by creating a childlike fantasy world. She decorated her cell walls with Mickey Mouse posters and her bed sheets with Sesame Street characters. A colour TV, toys and gifts furnished the rest of her abode. Karla dieted, worked out in the gym, plucked her eyebrows, manicured her fingernails, highlighted her hair and obsessed over her appearance. She took correspondence courses towards her BA, wore her own clothes, ate snacks from the prison canteen and received family visits at a cottage on the prison grounds. Her parents even brought her rottweiller, Buddy, for visits.

Karla wrote letters to her friends about Paul. 'I'm going through some difficult times dealing with the death of our relationship. That's how I'm going to treat it . . . like a death. I almost would rather have had him die because then at least I'd be able to grieve properly.' In another letter, 'I'm, going to sue Paul for the return of all my clothes and other stuff – TV, VCR and dining room set. I'm not going to let him have everything.'

With the closure of the Kingston penitentiary, Karla was transferred to a 15-million-dollar medium security prison in Joliette, Quebec where inmates are permitted to do their own cooking and cleaning. The prison, dubbed 'Club Fed', looks more like a holiday retreat than a prison. Instead of guards and cells, there are cottages with porch swings. Instead of bars, there are venetian blinds. The grounds are landscaped with flowers, maple and oak trees and manicured lawns. Although Karla became eligible for parole in 1998, she made no attempt to apply for parole and denied reports that she'd already been home on unescorted weekend day passes.

Karla knew that her real sentence would begin when her jail term ended.

July 4, 2005

Serial killer, Karla Homolka was released from prison on July 4th 2005 after serving only 12 years for the rapes and murders of three teenage girls, including her younger sister — who she offered to her rapist husband as a virginity gift. 'She is paralyzed with fear, completely panicked,' said Christian Lachance, one of her attorneys. 'When I saw her, she was in a state of terror, almost in a trance. She cannot conceive of what her life will be like outside.'

One thing is certain, though. With the international release of the movie, *Karla*, there will be nowhere to hide.

7

TWENTY WHACKS

The last place a woman wants to
pickaxe a man to death is Texas.
It's the equivalent of a black
man raping a white woman in
civil war Georgia.

Not all women who rape and kill are compliant victims and
accomplices to coercive men. One of the most ruthless and
sadistic serial sex killers of all time, was a sixteenth-century
Countess named Elisabeth Bathory of Hungary. Thirty-five
witness testimonies from a four year inquest described the
moonlit orgies, the sadistic tortures and the cannibalistic
sexuality practised by Countess Bathory inside her castle walls.
Bathory's castles housed custom designed torture devices
including a thick rounded club of polished wood carved in the
shape of a phallus and the dreaded 'iron maiden', a form-fitting
coffin-like cage lined with spikes. Nicknamed 'The Blood
Countess', Elisabeth Bathory reportedly tortured, sexually
assaulted and bludgeoned to death an estimated six hundred
and fifty virgin women, most of them servants girls, and then
bathed in their blood. She believed that by bathing in the blood
of virgins, she would preserve her youthful beauty. The moats
to her castles were choked with cadavers when she was finally

arrested and thrown in prison where she eventually died in 1613.

Almost three centuries later in Fall River, Massachusetts, another female killer with a penchant for blood gained notoriety after she chopped up her father and stepmother with 81 whacks from an axe. For nearly a hundred years, children memorialized her by skipping rope and chanting a morbid jingle to the tune of 'Ta Ra Ra Boom De Ay'.

> Lizzie Borden took an ax
> and gave her mother 40 whacks
> And when she saw what she had done
> she gave her father 41.

With the dawn of a new millennium, children are no longer skipping rope and chanting. They're smoking dope and rapping.

> Karla Tucker took a pick ax
> and gave some motherfucker twenty big whacks
> And when she saw what she had done
> She grinned and climaxed just for fun

HUNTSVILLE, TEXAS

23 February 1998. Karla Faye Tucker was scheduled to die by lethal injection. Pope John Paul II, Jerry Falwell, Pat Robertson and thousands of born-agains prayed for her life to be spared. Some called her 'a paradox of evil and saintliness'. Journalist Bob Harris called her 'a foxy looking, Bible thumping, artery slashing double murderer who wanted clemency because she recently found God . . . The only reason anyone gave a ding-

dang about this woman was because she was really cute which gave the TV cameras something to point at.'

HAND-ME-DOWN JOHNS

Karla Faye Tucker was cute alright. She was a cute, feisty tomboy who grew up in Houston, Texas, wore shit-kicker boots and knew how to use them. Her mother, Carolyn, was a homemaker, an alcoholic and a drug addict with a red hot temper, a foul mouth and an appetite for trouble. Carolyn scolded her girls into keeping a clean and tidy house, minding their manners and 'doing as I say, not as I do'. She told them they were sitting on a gold mine, that their 'snatches' would pay the bills and get them everything they ever wanted in life.

Karla's father, Larry Tucker, worked as a longshoreman and was part owner of a boat dealership. 'Daddy just loved mother so dadgum much,' recalled Karla. Unfortunately, Carolyn didn't share Karla's amorous enthusiasm for Larry. She believed that rules were made to be broken and that included her wedding vows. Anyone could see that Karla wasn't Larry's biological daughter. Karla had black hair. Larry had reddish hair. Karla had Greek features. Larry had anglo features. Carolyn finally admitted to Karla that her real father was a Greek fireman but Karla covered her ears with her hands and wouldn't listen. As far as she was concerned, Larry was her dad.

Although she was an academic failure, Karla was no air-head. Her teachers told her she had the aptitude to be an A student but Karla hated school and she hated people telling her what to do – and that included her teachers. She'd show up at school loaded and get suspended for falling asleep in class or fist fighting. Like her mother, she was hot tempered, rebellious and unmanageable. 'I wanted to have my own way of doing things . . . I wanted to be the first female quarterback in the NFL.'

It was an ugly divorce. Larry called Carolyn a 'bitch' and a 'whore' and accused her of running around with pimps and crooks and underworld types. The courts determined that Carolyn was an unfit mother and awarded Larry custody of eight-year-old Karla and her two sisters. Carolyn warned Larry in no uncertain terms 'Lay one hand on my girls and I'll take you to court.'

By the age of nine, Karla was already smoking pot. 'Everybody was doing it – older kids, my sisters, kids my age.' When she proved to be too big a handful for Larry, he called his ex-wife. Carolyn was a perfectionist who knew exactly how to handle her daughter's dope habit. 'If you're going to smoke, little lady, you're going to do it right,' she scolded with a Texas drawl. Carolyn handed Karla some rolling papers and made her roll joints until she got it right. 'Mother was like that . . . if you were going to do something, you had to do it right. That's why I've always been able to roll a joint just perfect.' Karla worshipped her mother like she was the Virgin Mary. She bragged about how close they were – so close that 'we used to share drugs like lipstick.' By age 11, Karla graduated from pot to heroin. She loved the needle. 'I got as much out of the needle going in as I did the drug.' That was the one big difference between Karla and her mother. Carolyn hated needles. When she couldn't stick the needle in right, she'd get Karla to do it for her.

Following in her mother and sister's footsteps, Karla started turning tricks for a living at the ripe old age of 13. She was the youngest in the family which meant she got the hand-me-downs. But Karla didn't get hand-me-down clothes or hand-me-down toys. She got hand-me-down needles and hand-me-

164

down johns. Mamma Tucker passed her tricks on to Karla's sister, Kari, who passed them on to Karla.

Karla had a reputation as a sex-crazed nymphomaniac – a girl who could never get enough. Between tricks, she dated beer-bellied bikers, musicians and Vietnam vets. The vets taught her military combat techniques. The bikers taught her how to build Harley choppers. The musicians taught her to be a roadie. Between the ages of 13 and 15, Karla travelled on and off with the Allman Brothers Band and scored with Gregg Allman and Dicki Betts. Like her mother, Karla drank, drugged, fornicated and partied hard with the best and the worst of them – rock'n'rollers, roadies, Green Berets and outlaws.

Karla met Stephen Griffith at age 19 and married him. She got off the drugs for awhile and lived a half normal life. On Christmas Eve 1979, Carolyn Tucker died of a stroke in a public hospital after several bouts with hepatitis. Karla was devastated. 'She died when I was twenty and I don't know, it changed me. I turned stone cold to the world . . . I idolized my mother something fierce . . . my whole life was shattered that day.'

WIMPS AND HE-MEN

Karla got bored with married life. She left her new husband and moved into a rented apartment at Quay Point with her best friend, Shawn, who turned tricks for a living. Karla knew she could make a quick fifteen hundred selling her butt in Midland, so that's what she did. After a hard week's work, Karla was anxious to get home and enjoy a good night's sleep. When she returned to her apartment, she found a leaky Harley-Davidson leaning on its kick stand in the middle of the living room with black oil dripping into a puddle on the rug. Karla peered through the bedroom door and saw the hairy ass owner of the bike humping her friend Shawn. His name was Jerry Lynn Dean and it was 'hate' at first sight. He was a short, wimpy looking, foul smelling, 26-year-old low life with glasses and long, dirty blond hair. Karla booted Jerry's hairy ass and leaky Harley out the door.

Biker chicks like he-men and Karla Faye Tucker was a bona fide biker chick. Jerry Lynn Dean was a bona fide 'poor excuse for a man'. The two didn't mix. He-men are tough enough to get the heads of their dicks tattooed. When Jerry Lynn made the mistake of showing up again at Karla's apartment to ball her best friend Shawn and drip black oil on her rug for a second time, Karla kicked him out and told him to stay the hell out. Jerry split, took Shawn with him and married her. Karla and Shawn remained friends.

Danny Garrett was a real man. He was so manly that he had a fly tattooed onto the tip of his penis and carried a .38 caliber pistol in a holster in one boot and drugs in the other boot. Danny was a war vet who worked as a Houston bartender. He bragged about serving in Nam with the baby-killers but people who really knew him said he'd only been a medic in the Philippines. When Danny first laid eyes on Karla Faye, he was slouched in a chair in the reception room of a doctor's office waiting for a prescription. Karla strolled in wearing skin-tight jeans, a black T-shirt and shit kicker boots. She was 105 pounds, trim and muscular. Danny was broad shouldered and hulkish looking with reddish-brown hair like her dad. To make a good impression, Danny told Karla stories about killing 'gooks' in Vietnam and about how he had been part of an elite assassination squad that was so top secret, it wasn't even on his service record. He told her that killing people was a money making proposition and that he worked for the mob. He said he wanted to 'off' his ex-wife, Phyllis, and save a couple of her fingers for souvenirs. Danny offered to train Karla to be the first female 'hit man' in the Mafia. He could teach her night vision and show her how to carry a gun, how to jump fences wearing a ski mask and how to become a predator instead of prey. Danny was Karla's kind of man. He did wild and crazy things that she thought only happened in Charles Bronson movies.

Danny and Karla glommed onto each other like mozzarella cheese and they rented a three bedroom 'tract' house on McKean Street in northern Houston. Danny owned a couple of shotguns and kept one hidden behind the couch in the living room in case of trouble. Karla's older sister, Kari, moved in with Karla and Danny and so did Karla's schizophrenic pit bulls, Tooter and Tessa. The McKean house became a revolving door of dopers and deadbeats coming and going, moving in and moving out, crashing for the night, fornicating like jack-hammers and consuming an endless supply of booze, drugs, junk food and movie rentals. Danny and Karla liked murder and war movies. Their favourite was a mystery thriller called *Eye Of The Needle* in which Donald Sutherland stars as a Nazi hit man who kills without emotion and kills instantly. It struck a nerve for Danny and Karla who watched it over and over again.

By the the ripe old age of 23 Karla Faye Tucker was already a veteran prostitute, a junkie and a would-be assassin, living in violent subculture with an adopted family of bikers and addicts. She was like the God of McKean street. Any father who crossed her or messed with the people she cared about were dead meat.

A SACRILEGE

March 1983. It was three months before the murders. Karla Faye persuaded Shawn (still married to Jerry Lynn Dean) to go to New Orleans with her and party with a rock and roll band.

Jerry resented Karla's control over Shawn. He resented her threats to his masculinity and he resented the way she publicly humiliated and embarrassed him. To get even, Jerry Lynn took a knife and slashed some photographs inside Karla's photo album that Shawn was keeping for her. When Karla found out that Jerry had desecrated her beloved mother's image, she became unhinged. Nobody got away with that. Karla tore after Jerry like a prizefighter at the sound of the bell. She delivered a crushing blow to his face, shattered his glasses and sent him to the hospital. The doctors had to extract slivers of glass from Jerry's eyeball. Karla really knew how to hurt a guy.

The McKean Street family was getting as big as the Waltons. Kari's ex-husband, Ronnie Burrell, moved in to the house and went into business with Jimmy Liebrant making speed. Shawn moved into a room with Kari after Jerry Lynn Dean busted her nose and punched her in the mouth. Karla, Kari and Shawn, turned tricks together, partied together and had sex together – threesomes, foursomes, switching and swapping. One week's work netted them an average of 2,000 bucks a piece.

Except for her father, Danny Garrett may have been one of the only men Karla ever loved. He asked her to marry him and he asked her to stop turning tricks for a living because 'You can't be in love and do that stuff'. Karla assured him she'd never cheated on him. She explained that tricks weren't the same thing as cheating because tricks were business. Karla was devastated when she found out Danny had cheated on her. To make things worse, he cheated on her with her own sister, Kari. Instead of getting mad, Karla clammed up and became mute. The people she loved most in the world, had crossed her. She didn't know how to deal with it. Danny regretted the affair. 'I don't think Karla ever trusted me after that.'

When Karla finally broke the silence, and got mad – but not at Danny and Kari. She got mad at Jerry Dean instead. Jerry had committed two cardinal sins. He had injured her dead mother's memory and he had rearranged her best friend's face. Karla wanted to get even and have a little fun at Jerry's expense, so, she and Shawn and Kari dressed up in hats, sunglasses and disguises, then headed for the ATM machine. With their identities safely concealed from the instant teller camera, the trio withdrew $460 cash and cleaned out Jerry's bank account using a bank card that Shawn had taken from Jerry when she left him. When Jerry discovered his zero bank account balance, he put two and two together and threatened to file charges. On second thought, he decided to put out a contract on Karla Faye Tucker.

Rumours were flying about Jerry's contract on Karla Faye – not to kill her but to burn her with a flare gun and scar her for life. Everybody knew Jerry kept a flare gun on top of his TV but Karla figured Jerry was too 'chicken-shit' to ever do something that violent on his own. He'd have to pay somebody else to do his dirty work for him. Somebody like Sideburns. It was rumoured that Sideburns and his biker buddies had agreed to get the job done for 300 bucks. Like a bad case of the flu, the 'he-said-she-said' talk travelled back and forth until both sides appeared ready to rumble.

BIRTHDAY ORGY

From Friday 10 June until Sunday 12 June 1983, Karla, Danny and Jimmy Liebrant shot crystal, drank tequila and ate pills like they were M & Ms. 11 June was Kari's birthday, which gave everybody a great excuse to party. Karla partied for three days without sleep. Streams of people came and went in a blur. Shawn, Kari, Jimmy and a drop-in male got into some kinky four-way sex and videotaped it. For the entire weekend, people binged on sex and a home-made smorgasbord of valium, percodan, mandrax, dilaudid and methadone mixed with heroin, tequila, rum and marijuana. Karla was out of sexual commission with an ovarian cyst and had to pass on tricks and orgies that weekend. Danny, who was recovering from hepatitis, also abstained. Both were bored and agitated. They'd been indoors all weekend getting smashed on an alcohol and drug feeding frenzy and their nerves were shot. 'We were very wired and we was looking for something to do,' recalled Karla. To combat the boredom, Karla, Danny and Jimmy Liebrant talked about stealing motorcycle parts from Jerry Lynn Dean's bike. They could use the parts for the Harley chopper that Karla was building. Just for the hell of it, Danny started drawing the floor plan to Jerry's apartment. He'd been to his apartment before, knew the layout and was game to go case the joint. He called it a 'reconnaissance mission' – like in Nam. Karla went and got a set of keys to Jerry's apartment which she'd found in Shawn's jeans while she was doing the laundry.

LIKE GI JANE AND JOE

Karla, Danny and Jimmy were flying high on speed, pills, tequila and Jack Daniels as they filed out the door on the night of 12 June 1983. Danny, wearing a black T-shirt with a Harley Eagle on the front, grabbed a shotgun on his way out. The high octane trio piled into Danny's 1977 blue Ranchero pick-up truck and burned rubber down McKean street on their 'reconnaissance mission'. The Ranchero pulled around to the back of a generic-looking apartment building in a red-neck neighborhood. There were no lights on in the building. Jimmy parked and waited outside in the Ranchero while Karla and Danny, with shotgun in

170

hand, circled around to the front. Danny had schooled Karla in military combat techniques and this was her big chance to show off. Like *G.I. Jane*, Karla crept up to the door, inserted the key into the lock of Jerry's ground floor apartment and opened up.

WAR GAMES

Jerry was a light sleeper. He heard noises and sprung up into a sitting position. 'What's going on?' he shouted, hoping the noises were just his imagination. Silence. In a half crouch position, Danny blindly weaved his way through the dark toting his shotgun and using the night vision that he'd learned in the military. Karla shadowed him through the kitchen and edged her way along a hallway leading to Jerry's bedroom.

Jerry's room was blacked out except for a sliver of light angling through the curtained window. The room was cluttered with junk – mostly work tools, step ladders and scaffolding. Karla followed Danny inside Jerry's bedroom. She saw Jerry sitting naked on a futon mattress on the floor. 'I could see the silhouette of a body that had sat up . . . I could see the outline of everything . . . and I walked past Danny and sat down on top of him . . . ' Straddling Jerry Lynn Dean, Karla yelled, 'Move and you're dead, motherfucker!' Jerry pleaded with her, 'We can work it out.' Jerry tried bucking Karla off but she rode him like a bronco and struggled with him as he gripped her arms above the elbows. Danny reached for a claw hammer and smashed Jerry's skull with it, knocking him face down to the floor, before leaving the room to score some motorcycle parts from Jerry's bike.

Karla could hear gurgling noises like a backed-up carburetor. She flicked on the bedroom light. The gurgling noises were coming from Jerry's lungs and throat and they were making her crazy. She saw a 15-pound pickaxe leaning against the bedroom wall next to the bed. Karla hoisted it up over her head and drove the two-foot blade into Jerry's torso like she was splitting wood. Jerry had pissed her off. He pissed her off when he leaked motor oil onto her carpet. He pissed her off when he stabbed the photographs of her deceased mother. He pissed her off when he busted her best friend's face. And he especially pissed her off when he threatened to put out a contract to burn and scar her for life. As Karla buried the pick into Jerry's body, she felt a sexual rush. With every thrust of the pick, Karla paid back a thousand thrusting dicks, a thousand thrusting tricks that had bought and used her body like a urinal from the time she was 13.

Jimmy Leibrant was waiting outside in the Ranchero. He got bored and came inside the apartment to help Danny load motorcycle parts into the flat bed of the truck. Jimmy noticed a sucking sound coming from Jerry Lynn Dean's bedroom. He went to investigate, peered through the bedroom doorway and saw Karla furiously picking away at Jerry's torso like she was tenderizing meat. The pickaxe got hooked inside Jerry's back. Karla put one foot on his torso, choked the pickaxe handle with her hands and tried wriggling it loose. When the blood-soaked pick finally jerked free, Karla lifted it up over her head again. She momentarily glanced sideways at Jimmy who was standing wide-eyed in the doorway. He watched her as she 'smiled and hit the dude again'. Jimmy spun around and bolted out of the apartment and down the street like he was being chased by Godzilla.

When Danny returned to the bedroom, Karla complained about the gurgling noise. She couldn't make it go away. Danny rolled Jerry's gored and mangled body over – face up. He raised the pickaxe over his head and plunged the blade down into Jerry's chest. The gurgling noise stopped and the room fell dead silent. Danny returned to the task at hand – stealing motorcycle parts for Karla's chopper.

Karla saw something move over by the bedroom wall. That something turned out to be a body cringing on the floor under a blanket. She hadn't noticed it before. The person was hiding their head under a pillow and they were shaking uncontrollably. Karla reached for the pickaxe, aimed the blood red blade at the covered body and swung. The pick glanced off the person's shoulder. 'I tried again the second time,' recalled Karla, 'and when I did the person came up from under the covers and it was the woman and she grabbed at the pickaxe.' The woman was Deborah Thornton, a 32-year-old married bookkeeper who Jerry had met at a party earlier that night. Thornton, who was taller and heavier than Karla, begged for her life as she wrestled with Karla for control of the axe. Karla swung again.

Danny heard the scuffle, raced into the bedroom and took possession of the axe. Deborah Thornton had seen everything. She had to be eliminated. While Danny took care of business, Karla went and loaded boxes into the truck. When she got back, she saw what looked like a badly-scripted scene from a suspense thriller. The pickaxe was protruding from Deborah's shoulder and instead of pleading for her life, she was now pleading to be killed – quickly. 'Oh God, it hurts. If you're going to kill me, please hurry up,' she begged as she tried prying the pickaxe out of her shoulder. Danny obliged. He kicked Deborah in the head, dislodged the axe from her shoulder and after several more thrusts, sunk the two-foot blade into her chest and heart, seven inches deep. 'She was a tough motherfucker to kill,' Karla told her sister later. Killing someone wasn't supposed to be that hard. She'd watched *Eye Of The Needle* four times. Donald Sutherland made it look so easy.

Karla and Danny busied themselves carrying the motorcycle frame out of the apartment and loading it into Jerry's 1974 El Camino. It was already 6.30 in the morning. The sun was coming up. With their reconnaissance mission accomplished, Danny and Karla split in different directions – Danny in the Ranchero, Karla in the stolen El Camino.

DOUBLE HOMICIDE

Gregory Travers worked with Jerry Lynn Dean installing alarms for a security company. When Jerry Lynn didn't pick him up for work that morning in the El Camino, Gregory figured he must've overslept. He went to Jerry's apartment to wake him up. When he looked inside the bedroom, he knew Jerry was never going to wake up ever again. Jerry's naked body was cratered with holes and a woman was laying by the wall with a pickaxe sticking out of her heart. The entire bedroom looked like a butcher's chopping block. Blood and guts were splattered everywhere. Gregory reported to the police that he'd found Jerry Lynn Dean's perforated body on the bedroom floor, 'and I seen the girl with the pickaxe in her heart'. Their bodies were riddled with more than 20 axe wounds.

The next afternoon, while the McKean Street clan sat around watching TV, a special news report described the grisly pickaxe double murders. Everybody watched Jerry's body being carted out of his apartment in a body bag. Karla got up, pointed at the TV screen and yelled, 'That's the motherfucker!'

Karla and Danny covered their tracks and disposed of the stolen bike parts. Kari overheard them talking about snuffing out people who might testify against them – people like Jimmy Liebrant and Ronnie Burrell. A month went by without any arrests and Karla and Danny started boasting about getting away with murder.

174

THICKER THAN WATER

Kari moved out of the house on McKean Street and took Tessa, the pit bull, with her. She became live-in lovers with Danny's brother, Douglas Garrett, who she'd been seeing off and on for awhile. Both Kari and Douglas feared for their lives and decided to turn their brother and sister in to the police. They contacted homicide detective, J.C. Mosier. Douglas told Mosier point blank that his brother, Danny Garrett, and Kari's sister, Karla Faye Tucker, murdered Jerry Lynn Dean and Deborah Thornton. Douglas quoted Karla as saying, 'I come with every stroke.' Kari confirmed that her sister told her the same thing. 'She told me that every time that she had picked Jerry that she looked up and grinned and got a nut (sexual orgasm) and picked him again.' Mosier insisted that the only way they were ever going to nail Karla and Danny was to get incriminating statements from them. Mosier asked Douglas if he was willing to wear a wire. Douglas thought it over and agreed.

The cops outfitted Douglas Garrett with a transmitter taped to his chest and a reel to reel tape recorder hidden in his boot. They told him to just act natural, make small talk at first and to use the code word, 'Jesus Christ', if he got into trouble. Mosier instructed Garrett to try and get a taped admission from Karla that she was sexually turned on by the murders so that the prosecution could use her statement in evidence.

With arrest warrants in hand, Houston Police officers parked in an unmarked police van on a side street near the McKean house with listening devices. They listened as Douglas Garrett entered the house. They heard the chatter of people in the living room as Douglas strolled in – Ronnie Burrell, Jimmy Liebrant's sister, Marla, and a girl named Cookie were hanging out. Douglas snapped open a beer and nonchalantly strolled into Karla and

Danny's bedroom. Danny was getting ready for work and Karla was lounging on the bed eating pills like they were peanuts. Douglas made small talk at first. The small talk soon turned to leading questions and to the incriminating answers that the cops had been waiting for.

> DOUGLAS: Did y'all go over there with it in mind to kill them people? . . . Were them people asleep? . . . Did you wake them up?
>
> DANNY: It was a freak thing . . . We just freaked out.

Douglas asked Karla why she used a pickaxe.

> KARLA: It was there. It was just there.
>
> DOUGLAS: Tell me something, Karla. Is it true you got sexual gratification?
>
> KARLA: (bragging) Well, hell yes.

Douglas told them how worried he was about the cops snooping around.

> KARLA: (confidently) They're just digging. They ain't got shit.
>
> DANNY: They got nothing, Doug. No fingerprints. Nothing.

Douglas assured Karla and Danny of his loyalty.

> DOUGLAS: You know I'm your brother and I'll take care of you.

176

THE BUST

Danny was late for work and split. Karla walked Douglas outside, patted him affectionately on the back and told him to stop worrying. Everything was cool. Karla strolled back inside the house and snacked on fried fish and ketchup as Douglas mounted his bike and thundered away.

Beverly Lowry, who researched the case and visited Karla Faye Tucker on death row, described Karla's arrest in her book, *Crossed Over*. 'With guns drawn, the police push the door open – "Police! Don't move!" – and everybody starts screaming, yelling, policemen all over the house, everybody afraid of getting shot. Tooter (Karla's pit bull) is shut up in the bedroom barking her head off and one of the policemen is shouting, "Will this goddamn dog bite?" and Karla's saying, "Don't shoot the dog, please don't shoot the dog," and Cookie is saying, "I'll take Tooter outside, please don't shoot the dog," because they both know if the police open the bedroom door and storm in, Tooter will attack and they will kill her. The next thing Karla knows, she's face-down against the wall and ketchup and fish are flying all over the place and there's a big gun at her temple.'

In hindsight, Karla shook her head and laughed about the arrest. It was like a bad episode from 'Cops'. 'I see these television shows where people get arrested and it's embarrassing, you know? Because it happens just like that. I don't know, ketchup all over the place. They kicked my feet apart, patted me down . . .'

WELL HELL, YES

In the courtroom, Karla Faye Tucker wore 'little-girl puffed sleeves' and a white plastic jailhouse cross. She was cute, petite and innocent looking – too childlike and too helpless looking to be anything but the compliant victim of a battering boyfriend or husband. But the disarming image didn't fit the voice of the woman making incriminating statements on tape. The jury listened as prosecutor, Joe Magliolo, played back the secretly recorded evidence that Douglas Garrett had turned over to police. They listened to the crude and cocky voice of a woman who had overpowered a male biker and his female companion, punched holes in them like coffee cards and got sexually buzzed by her own violence. Searching for a stereotype explanation of Tucker's unfeminine behaviour, the prosecution turned to the 'vengeful whore' label.

Douglas Garrett, who married Karla's sister, Kari, one week before the trial, stepped up onto the witness stand. He testified that, in his opinion, there was only one explanation for why his brother and his wife's sister committed such an evil crime. The devil made them do it. When it was Kari's turn to take the stand, she pointed her finger at Karla in the courtroom and identified her. 'That's her. That's the one.' Karla's gut balled up into a knot. Her own sister was pointing at her. Her own flesh and blood had snitched on her and was now delivering her to death row on a silver platter. 'Danny and Karla was proud of theirself,' testified Kari with a nasal twang. 'She didn't act remorse . . . they were giggling and smiling and saying they were famous . . . we were scared for our lives.' Most women know better than to raise their hand to a man in Texas let alone pickaxe a man to death. It's the equivalent of a black man raping a white woman in Civil War Georgia. Karla was given two generic court appointed attorneys – Henry Oncken and Mack Arnold. Henry Oncken was convinced that 'our only chance to save her was to try to humanize her. And the only way we could do that was to let her tell her story.' Arnold and

Oncken knew that putting Karla on the stand was a dangerous calculated risk – but a risk worth taking. Karla swore to tell the whole truth and nothing but the truth so help her God and God help her, that's exactly what she did. The prosecution pounced on her unrehearsed story like a hungry shredding machine.

In their closing arguments, it appeared as though Karla's defense lawyers had given up and thrown in the towel. Although they had advised Karla to enter a not guilty plea, they made no effort to contest the evidence against her and even agreed with the prosecution's case against her. It was as though Karla's own attorneys were delivering the closing arguments for the prosecution. It was as though her lawyers had turned against her just like Kari, Douglas, Jimmy and the others had done. Mack Arnold asked the jury for a guilty verdict against his client. 'The evidence is overwhelming that my client is guilty of capital murder and I think it would be an injustice for you to arrive at any other verdict . . . I don't think there's any doubt in my mind, in Henry Oncken's mind, or in Karla Faye Tucker's mind what the verdict is going to be.'

Mack Arnold proceeded to tell the jury that even if Danny Garrett struck the first blow, Karla was 'guilty' and even if she was high on drugs and didn't know what she was doing, she was 'guilty'. Arnold justified his summation as a calculated risk strategy 'to gain credibility with the jurors'. He acknowledged Karla's guilt, asked for a guilty verdict but appealed to the jury to spare her life. Because of her lawyers' initial advice to enter a plea of 'not guilty', Karla was facing a death sentence instead of life in prison. The calculated risks backfired.

Karla's confession of experiencing sexual orgasms with every stroke of the pickaxe was as pivotal to the prosecution's case against her as the murder weapon itself. The defense team made no effort to discount or discredit Karla's confession as 'idle tough talk' to impress her peers. With no objection from the defense, 'Well, hell yes' became the statement that put Karla on death row and sealed her doom. That statement was so powerful, in fact, that the prosecution chose to use it as the closing statement in their closing arguments to the jury. 'Does Karla Faye Tucker deserve the death penalty?' asked prosecutor Joe Magliolo as he stood before the jury. 'I'll let her answer that for herself.' Magliolo then punched the play button on the audio cassette player. The jury heard Karla's recorded voice boom into the courtroom with a resounding, 'Well, hell yes.' That answer had been Karla's response to a question that Douglas Garrett asked her while he was secretly taping their conversation for the police – 'Tell me something, Karla, is it true that you got sexual gratification?' Even though the prosecution exploited Karla's confession of being sexually turned-on during the commission of the assault, she was never charged with sexual assault.

SLAM DUNK

It was a 'slam dunk'. Prosecutors had turned brother and sister against brother and sister. They had secured witness deals, color photographs, videotapes, audiotapes and confessions. It took the jury only three hours of deliberation to decide the fate of Karla Faye Tucker and return a guilty verdict and a 'yes' for the death penalty. Karla had retaliated against male aggression in the jockstrap capital of America without shedding a tear or making excuses for her 'unfeminine' behaviour. She refused to conform to stereotyped prejudices about her gender or to play the naive, helpless, coerced victim. She proved beyond a reasonable doubt that a woman can be equally as tough and equally as malevolent as a man. 'I don't think any of this would've happened if my mother hadn't died,' added Karla, '. . . not that I blame Mother, I don't blame nobody but myself, but when she died, I don't know . . . my whole life was shattered that day . . .' Karla didn't blame the woman she'd 'shared drugs with like lipstick'. She didn't blame child abuse and she didn't blame Danny or drugs or post traumatic stress disorder or any other disorder. She blamed nothing and no one but herself.

Danny Garrett was tried and convicted of the capital murder of Deborah Thornton for driving a pickaxe through her heart while she begged him to kill her and get it over with. He died in prison of liver disease.

MIRACLE ON DEATH ROW

Dubbed the 'pickaxe killer' by a Houston newspaper, 24-year-old Karla Faye Tucker was shackled from head to toe and transported in a prison van along Texas Highway 36 to Gatesville, Texas – only a half hour from the infamous town of Waco. Karla peered through the van window and saw Mountainview maximum security prison loom up on the horizon. Mountainview was home for death-row inmates and it would be Karla's home for the next 14 years. As the van braked to a stop at the security gates a cool Texas wind whistled through the razor wire and chain link fence that was patrolled by guards on horseback carrying rifles.

Dressed in prison whites and segregated from the main prison population, Karla was warehoused in a cubby hole death-row cell. Out of sheer boredom, she stole a Bible from the prison ministry. 'I didn't know what I was reading and before I knew it, I was in the middle of my floor on my knees and I was asking God to forgive me.'

With no johns to hustle, no needles to inject, no friends to protect and no he-men to impress, Karla became a model prisoner. While waiting for an appeal that could save her from lethal injection and certain death, Karla joined Bible studies, took school courses, worked out, practised yoga and walked 15 miles every day. She began reading and writing and following a 12 step program. She even married Dana Brown, the prison chaplain, by proxy but since conjugal visits were forbidden to death-row inmates, the newlyweds were separated by a pane of plexiglass and the marriage was never consummated. 'My main mission in life now,' declared Karla, 'is to love . . . people out there . . . to love murderers, dope fiends, nonbelievers, everyone. Without Christ, I wouldn't be able to do that . . . Love without having to get anything back. Without expecting to be loved in return. It isn't me doing the loving, really, it is the Christ in me. I am loving others with the love of Christ and in doing so I hope to bring others to Christ.' Karla especially wanted to save her father, Larry Tucker, who came to visit her on death row three times a year.

The sincerity of Karla's remorse and rehabilitation were undeniable to journalist Florence King, who wrote, 'At first I despised her because she was so "sweet" but then I discovered she really was sweet.' The woman who the prosecuting attorney had called, 'the personification of evil' and 'a woman you could never turn your back on', won the sympathy of death penalty hard-liners like the Christian Coalition. She became a poster girl for the anti-capital punishment groups. Karla was a paradox. A born-again sinner turned saint. A whore turned virgin. Jerry Falwell, Pat Robertson, the 700 Club and even the brother and sister of one of the victims campaigned to save her.

Sceptics and cynics didn't buy Karla's story about finding God on death row. They said she was just doing what girls in her profession did best – faking it. But those who really knew her knew she had a big heart. It was big enough to love her mother, her father, her best friend, her sister, her boyfriend and her two pit bulls. And it was big enough to love Jesus. For Karla, you could love your mother and help her shoot heroin. You could love your boyfriend and still turn tricks. You could love your best friend and pickaxe her husband to death. Love meant righting a wrong. Love meant defending the honour of the people you love. No matter how twisted, it was the kind of love that Karla had learned on the streets and from her role models.

In 1992, an Amended Petition for Writ of Habeas Corpus was filed claiming that Karla's constitutional rights had been violated on the grounds that she had ineffective counsel. The petition charged that certain mitigating factors like drug-induced temporary insanity should have been considered and that the jury was not allowed to hear testimony regarding deals made with the state by certain hostile witnesses that testified against her. The facts of the case showed that on the fateful night of Sunday, 12 June 1983, Karla Faye Tucker had no intentions of killing anybody. Unlike Danny Garrett who boasted about killing 'gooks' in Nam, Karla never killed anybody in her life. Unlike Danny, who was carrying a shotgun that night, Karla was not armed with any weapons. Danny drew the floor plans. Danny led the way. Once they were inside the apartment, Karla followed Danny into Jerry's bedroom. She didn't attack Jerry Lynn Dean with a weapon. She sat on his lap, all 105 pounds of her, and she got into a fist fight with the man who had put out a $300 contract to burn her and scar her for life. Karla attacked Jerry Lynn Dean with nothing more than her bare fists. It was Danny who spontaneously picked up a claw hammer and smashed Jerry Lynn Dean's skull with it. It was Danny's fatal blow that caused the gurgling noise, that caused blood to pour into Jerry's lungs and throat and caused him to aspirate and choke to death on his own blood. Danny Garrett killed Jerry Lynn Dean. Karla assaulted the doomed man without premeditation while she was in state of drug-induced psychosis and temporarily insane. She also assaulted Deborah Thornton in the same state of psychosis. If Karla's defense lawyers had defended instead of prosecuting her, she may have had a chance to 'live again' after being 'born again'.

The Texas Court of Criminal Appeals denied Karla the right to a new trial. In spite of the growing support from church and media celebrities to spare her life, the US Supreme Court refused to consider overturning the State's decision. On 18 January 1998, Karla sent a letter to President George W. Bush, then, Governor of Texas asking him for clemency. She was not asking for her release but for the opportunity to spend the rest of her life doing service work in custody. Excerpts from the letter were later published.

To George W. Bush

'I am in no way attempting to minimize the brutality of my crime. It obviously was very, very horrible and I do take full responsibility for what happened. I also know that justice and law demand my life for the two innocent lives I brutally murdered that night. If my execution is the only thing, the final act that can fulfill the demand for restitution and justice, then I accept that. I will pay the price for what I did in any way our law demands it.'

'I was advised by my attorneys to plead not guilty and I was trusting their legal expertise. They knew I murdered Jerry and Deborah. I did not lie to them about it. I am, in fact, guilty. Very guilty.'

'I used to try and blame my mother because she was my role model and she fashioned and shaped me into what I was at an early age. At 14 she took me to a place where there was all men and wanted to "school me" in the art of being a call girl. I wanted to please my mother so much. I wanted her to be proud of me. So instead of saying no, I just tried to do what she asked. The thing is, deep down inside I knew that what I was doing was wrong. It may have been the norm for the crowd I was in, but it was not the norm for decent, upstanding families.'

'I no longer try to lay the blame on my mother or on society . . . I don't blame drugs either. When I say that I was out of it on drugs the night I brutally murdered two people, I fully realize that I made the choice to do those drugs. Had I chosen not to do drugs, there would be two people still alive today. But I did choose to do drugs, and I did lose it, and two people are dead because of me.'

'I did not plan on going over there that particular night to go into that apartment to kill anyone. But that is beside the point. The fact is, we went there, we went into the apartment, we brutally murdered two precious people, and we left out of there and even bragged about what we did for over a month afterward.'

'It was in October, three months after I had been locked up, when a ministry came to the jail and I went to the services, that night accepting Jesus into my heart. When I did this, the full and overwhelming weight and reality of what I had done hit me. I began crying that night for the first time in many years, and to this day, tears are a part of my life.'

'I also wanted to try and send some money out to one of my victim's family members (it was for Deborah's son, for his schooling). When Ron Carlson came to me in 1992 and told me he had forgiven me for what I had done to his sister, I let him know I was trying to get some money to his nephew. He told me not to. I would only be hurting him if I did send the money to him. And he told me that his nephew would not receive the money from me anyway because he wanted nothing to do with me. I understand the pain and I did not push.'

'Fourteen years ago, I was part of the problem. Now I am part of the solution . . . I have purposed to do right for the last 14 years, not because I am in prison, but because my God demands this of me. I know right from wrong and I must do right.'

'I feel that if I were in here still in the frame of mind I got arrested in, still acting out and fighting and hurting others and not caring or trying to do good, I feel sure you would consider that against me. I don't really understand why you can't or won't consider my change for the good in my favour.'

'I don't really understand the guidelines for commutation of death sentences, but I can promise you this: If you commute my sentence to life, I will continue for the rest of my life in this earth to reach out to others to make a positive difference in their lives.'

'I see people in here in the prison where I am who are here for horrible crimes, and for lesser crimes, who to this day are still acting out in violence and hurting others with no concern for another life or for their own life. I can reach out to these girls and try and help them change before they walk out of this place and hurt someone else.'

'I am seeking you to commute my sentence and allow me to pay society back by helping others. I can't bring back the lives I took. But I can, if I am allowed, help save lives. That is the only real restitution I can give.'

Signed: *Karla Faye Tucker*

In an interview with *Talk* Magazine, George W. Bush mocked and made fun of the woman he decided to put to death. 'Please' Bush whimpers, imitating Karla Faye Tucker with his lips pursed in mock desperation, 'Don't kill me.'

THE COUNTDOWN

It's big news when a woman is executed – especially when the woman is attractive and photogenic with high cheekbones, a cascading black mane, eyes the color of Belgian chocolate, a sunny smile and a chipped tooth. It's big news when she commits the most unthinkable act of violence, using the most unthinkable weapon and pops a 'nut'. The tabloids embraced the 'Dead Woman Walking' story and welcomed Karla into their celebrity hall of fame. David Frost, CBS, Larry King Live and 20/20 wanted interviews. Geraldo covered the 'Count Down To Execution' with camera zoom-ins on the 'dewy-eyed, full lipped, tawny haired . . . pin-up-looking chick.'

Prior to her scheduled execution, Larry King interviewed Karla on death row where she was housed with seven other death row women. He asked her about the night of the murder.

LARRY: Did you enjoy the violence?

KARLA: . . . I was very excited about doing different, crazy violent things. Yes. It was a part of me that was used to fit in with the crowd I was hanging around . . . to be accepted.

LARRY: Did you walk around with any guilt?

KARLA: I not only didn't walk around without any guilt, I was proud of thinking that I had finally measured up to the big boys.

LARRY: Your boyfriend was proud of you?

KARLA: Yes. Isn't that sick? That's crazy.

LARRY: No guilt?

KARLA: None, none back then. I didn't . . . I didn't care about anybody. I didn't care about myself. I didn't place any value on myself or anybody else.

LARRY: Was it your idea?

KARLA: No, it wasn't.

When Larry King asked Karla about the gender issue, she called it more of a hindrance than a help.

KARLA: This gender issue is almost forcing their

hand to say, 'we're not going to let a woman get away with it and be spared'.

Huntsville, Texas is a town where the song of the mockingbird awakens the dawn and where tall oak trees arch over the walkways at the State University, where crime rates are low and church attendance is high. It is a town that has been named the most desirable place to live in Texas . . . unless you're on death row.

3 FEBRUARY 1998, 5.30 PM

Karla was readied for the gurney while the world's media camped outside on her doorstep. Camera crews, international news teams, Amnesty International representatives and victims rights advocates crowded into the town of Huntsville to chronicle the event. Restaurants were packed. Motel rooms were booked solid. Twelve hundred demonstrators both for and against the death penalty and 200 reporters came to Huntsville for the countdown to the historical event. Karla Faye Tucker would be the first woman to be executed in Texas since 1863 and the American Civil War. Five hundred women had been put to death in the United States since the time of the pilgrims when witchcraft was a capital offence. University frat boys wearing rebel flags treated the execution like a fox hunt. Townsfolk went to church and prayed. Others held vigils.

Karla claimed she was a changed woman. Before being strapped into the death chamber gurney in Huntsville, the 38-year-old born-again Christian said, 'I am going to be face to face with Jesus now.' Nothing short of a divine miracle could stop, the pretty, doe-eyed, poster girl from being executed by lethal injection. The day before the execution, even Pope John Paul II requested that Karla's life be spared.

189

Karla Faye Tucker really was a changed woman. Her last meal was a testament to that fact. Instead of ordering a greasy double cheeseburger, fries and gravy and chocolate-drenched ice cream, Karla ordered a vegetarian plate – a banana, a peach and a tossed green salad. Moments before the lethal mix of three drugs was injected into her arm, Karla Faye spoke her last words to Deborah Thornton's relatives who were present as witnesses at her execution. Richard Thornton, the victim's widower, who spent 14 years seeking retribution for his wife's murder was present as well as Thornton's brother, Ronald Carlson, who opposed the execution. Karla spoke her last words. 'I would like to say to all of you . . . that I am so sorry . . . I hope God will give you peace with this.' After witnessing Karla's death by lethal injection, Deborah's widower, Richard Thornton, declared, 'That was the best ten minutes of my life.'

Karla Faye Tucker was executed on 3 February 1998. She was buried in a graveyard for inmates who die in prison unclaimed. Did the criminal and social justice system fail her?

'Well, hell yes'.

8

AGAINST HIS WILL

'A man is more than a dildo.'
Germaine Greer

Mary Letourneau. Karla Homolka. Pamela Smart. Lorena Bobbitt. Karla Faye Tucker. The news media found it unfathomable that these harmless looking women could be sex criminals. How could women who look like the All American 'girl-next-door' be guilty of such 'unfeminine' crimes as rape and sexual assault? Hadn't they been schooled in the art of gender role conformity? Women don't rape and victimize. Women *get* raped and victimized.

Denial of women's capacity for sexual aggression is an age old cultural tradition. Whenever a 'wayward' woman gets out of line, an army of reporters dutifully rush to the scene to defend that tradition. Lorena Bobbitt didn't amputate her husband's penis out of anger or revenge. She was 'temporarily insane'. Karla Homolka didn't ram a wine bottle into her murder victim's anus forty times on videotape. She was coerced. Karla Faye Tucker didn't experience sexual orgasms as she pick axed her victims to death. She was a different 'born-again' person. Mary Letourneau and Pamela Smart didn't commit child rape with their underage male students. They were victims of cupid's arrow.

As the media rallied to transform the threatening images of these wayward females from wrongful 'victimizers' to rightful 'victims', somehow the real victims of their crimes got lost in the hype. Mary Letourneau, who compared her woman-boy relationship to *Titanic*'s Jack and Rose, was suddenly catapulted onto newsstand and supermarket shelves alongside Kate Winslet and Leonardo DiCaprio. Her lawyer was so inundated with television, film and book deal offers that he had to hire a special media manager. Pamela Smart's story became the subject of a best-selling novel and two movies. Karla Faye Tucker bid a heart-wrenching farewell to her Christian fan club on Pat Robertson's 700 Club as Geraldo competed for ratings with a 'countdown' to her execution. A tidal wave of true crime books about Karla Homolka and Paul Bernardo cascaded onto book store shelves. By contrast, Lorena Bobbitt who committed the world's biggest 'no-no', faded into obscurity. Male producers didn't want to risk giving other women ideas.

BEYOND BELIEF

When a man commits a sex crime, it's ordinary news. When a woman commits a sex crime, it's an extraordinary event. If the woman is also cute, sexy and stereotypically feminine, it's a movie-of-the week, it's a book deal and a front-page spread in the tabloid hall of fame. Like movie stars, these extraordinary women are pursued by reporters and cameras, by writers and movie producers, by fans and fan mail. They appear as guests on TV talk shows and entertainment news shows and their glossy photographs are juxtaposed next to movie stars at the supermarket check-out counters, on book store shelves and on newsstands. Their lives and their crimes are eroticized and dramatized, glamorized and sensationalized, immortalized and hence, 'legitimized'. 'Infotainment' (a media cocktail of real news spiked with surreal entertainment) rewards criminal behaviour by making celebrity superstars out of rapists and killers and forgotten statistics out of their victims.

In all but a few sensationalized cases, female criminals are rarely studied and are consequently invisible. The stories that are sensationalized by the media portray women criminals as freaks of nature who behave in extreme and irrational ways. Media coverage of the Bobbitt case depicted Lorena's story as high farce and Lorena as cartoonishly dangerous, irrational and temporarily insane instead of a battered woman who was justified in fighting back. Lorena's actions were described by the media as 'extreme', 'inhuman', 'unthinkable' and 'beyond belief' while John's marital rape and brutality was minimized, trivialized and normalized. Editors Alice Meyers and Sarah Wright observe that, 'News reports that demonize women who fight back, keep victims of spousal abuse trapped in a Catch-22: they are either blamed for not leaving or are blamed for retaliating, while the legal system they are supposed to rely on does not adequately safeguard their lives.'

What the press *doesn't* say can have just as powerful an impact on public opinion and perception as what it *does* say. Male perpetrated sex crimes are treated as common, daily occurrences in every major newspaper in every major city of the world. Lurid stories of male sexual predators successfully violating helpless female victims are as normal, ordinary and common place as the want ads. The daily message is that women are 'pushovers' and easy targets of sexual violation. This masculine bias in reporting creates a distorted public perception that women never fight back, resist or fight off their attackers. The truth is that women do resist. Women do fight back and women do sometimes injure and kill their attackers. Where are all the countless stories of the countless women who have successfully fought back and why have their stories not been reported?

LIFE, DEATH OR A HAND SLAP

Whether they are cute and famous or not-so-cute and anonymous, the judiciary's female-offender sentencing practices are as inconsistent as the national weather report. Sentencing extremes can be traced to chivalry justice and the often contradictory task of defending cultural tradition and, at the same time, setting standards of accountability. How can women be defended as non-aggressive, yet be held criminally accountable for their acts of aggression? Judicial options include dropping or renaming the charges and plea-bargaining reduced sentences for women who blame their aggression on coercive men.

Even though Pamela Smart confessed to sexually violating her underage student, she was never charged with statutory rape. Her refusal to plea-bargain the 'conspiracy to commit murder' charge and to play the weeping, repentant victim got her 'life without parole'. Lorena Bobbitt was not charged with 'sexual assault' for cutting off her husband's penis. The courts called it 'malicious wounding', but feminists called it 'petty larceny'. On the witness stand, Lorena was convincingly forgetful, recounted victim stories and wept her way to an acquittal. In spite of the videotaped evidence of Karla Homolka sadistically raping her murder victims, she was never charged with rape or sexual assault. She blamed the rapes and murders on her husband and plea-bargained a prison sentence that would qualify her for full parole in four years. Born-again Christian, Karla Faye Tucker, and every other female Texan learned that no woman ever raises her hand (or a pickaxe) to a man in Texas and

194

lives to brag about it. Mary Letourneau had the misfortune of appearing before a woman judge who put her behind bars, threw away the key and proved that a woman judge can't be accused of gender bias or sissy sentencing.

MEN ARE NOT DILDOS

Recent studies show that females are responsible for one third of the sexual abuse of boys under the age of 16. Underage victims of a sexual assault by an adult female are often unaware that the sexual seduction constitutes abuse. Female rapists explain that they are expressing 'love' or educating their victims about sex. They use tricks, bribes, blackmail and their position of authority to win victim cooperation. Statutory Rape is defined as 'the crime of having sexual intercourse even with consent with a person below the age of consent', which may be 16, 17 or 18 depending upon state statutes. By complaining about a female sexual attack, male victims run the risk of being labelled 'wimps' or 'queers' for not enjoying the experience. Their fear of being teased or disbelieved paralyses them into silence.

According to the FBI's Uniform Crime Report, 5,681 females were arrested for sex offenses other than forcible rape and prostitution in the United States in 1996. Two hundred and eighty-one females were arrested for forcible rape. These statistics are extremely misleading since sexual assault by females may rank as one of the most under reported of all criminal offenses.

The belief that it is impossible for a man to either have or maintain an erection when he is being sexually assaulted by a woman is a 'sexual myth', according to Yale sex researchers, William Masters, MD of the Masters and Johnson Institute and Phillip M. Sarrel, MD of the Yale School of Medicine. Although an involuntary erection and ejaculation can sometimes be triggered by fear, it is generally believed that if a man gets an erection when he is with a woman, he must want her – therefore, it can't be rape. According to Masters and Sarrel, 'Nothing is further from the truth . . . Like most other sexual myths, its general acceptance has exerted an unfortunate influence on medicine, psychology and the law. Men who are raped by a woman do not enjoy the experience. They are fearful, panicked, confused and extremely loath to admit the experience to anyone including their therapists. The few male victims who have come forward and talked to therapists about their experience exhibit the same symptoms as female rape victims including low self esteem, depression and rejection of intimacy.'

When computer design manager, Tom Sanders, accepted an invitation from his female boss to attend an after-hours office meeting, he got more than he bargained for. His boss offered him a glass of Chardonnay, then cornered him and demanded sexual favours with a 'no holds barred' frontal assault. Tom, a happily married man with kids, momentarily responded to her advances before screaming 'No!' Tom later charged his attacker with sexual harassment and graphically described what happened at a gender-war mediation hearing.

TOM: She took the phone from me and she kissed me.

LAWYER: Where?

TOM: She kissed me in my ear, on my neck, on my mouth. She put her tongue in my mouth.

LAWYER: When you asked her to stop, did she?

TOM: No. She unzipped my pants and she massaged my penis.

LAWYER: Were you aroused?

TOM: Yes. Then she slid down and she put my penis in her mouth.

LAWYER: Did you climax?

TOM: I grabbed her by the wrists. I threw her on the ground. I just wanted to get out of there.

LAWYER: And at that point, what did Miss Johnson do?

TOM: She said, 'You're dead'.

Tom is then questioned by the lawyer for the accused.

DEFENSE: Do you admit having an erection during the course of your meeting?

TOM: She had her top open. It was an involuntary reflex.

DEFENSE: Do you admit putting your erect penis in her mouth?

TOM: She did it.

DEFENSE: (sarcastically) Oh . . . I forgot.

This scene is from the movie *Disclosure*, a steamy sex thriller starring Michael Douglas and Demi Moore. Both male and female viewers of 'Disclosure' felt the movie stretched credibility by suggesting that a red-blooded heterosexual American male wouldn't beg, roll over, play dead and walk barefoot across hot coals for a chance to be sexually assaulted by the sleek and sensuous Demi Moore.

Rape expert, Nicholas Groth, reports that the chances of a female rapist being prosecuted are practically nil. 'We've seen these guys forcibly assaulted by women, but they get in front of the police or courts, and who's going to believe them?' Warren Farrell, author of *The Myth of Male Power*, points out that 'the female equivalent of having an erection is being vaginally lubricated' but a man can't use the female equivalent excuse against a rape charge by saying, 'Yes, your Honour, she did say "no", but she was lubricated, so obviously she wanted it and therefore it isn't rape.'

'Female rape or attempted rape by force or threat of force is not a new phenomenon,' says criminologist Ronald B Flowers. 'During a certain time in our country's history, a white woman in the south could force a black man to have sexual intercourse with her by threatening to scream "rape". Since the mere accusation could cost the black man his life, this incident would certainly qualify as rape by the very real threat of bodily harm.'

Masters and Sarrel collected clinically documented evidence of the rape of four men on separate occasions by one or more women under threat of violence or death. In spite of documented case histories of men being sexually assaulted by women, such cases are rarely reported in the scientific literature. The perception of women as rapists runs contrary not only to popular belief but to the legal definition of rape itself. In American courtrooms, for sexual assault to qualify as felonious rape, there must be 'forcible penetration of the vagina by a penis, however slight'. Rape, as the current law defines it, is the forcible perpetration by an act of sexual intercourse on the body of a woman not one's wife. This antiquated definition categorizes women as *victims* of rape, men as the perpetrators of rape and the penis as a special weapon of rape. It exempts men from prosecution who have sexual intercourse with their wives without their consent, yet 50 states have now made marital rape a crime. Contrary to the legal definition, hundreds of women are arrested every year for forcible rape. In seven states, men have no legal recourse against their female attackers since women are entirely excluded from state statutes.

Female serial rapist, Rosemary West, used a vibrator with which to rape her victims. Karla Homolka used a wine bottle. For male rapists, the favourite weapon of choice is the penis but many have been known to use sticks, bottles and fingers as invasive tools to invade the vagina and other orifices. Forced oral or rectal penetration using an object is as much a violation of the personal, private inner space of a human being as vaginal penetration by a penis. Rape is an assault to the body. If the justice system is to rid itself of masculine bias, a gender-neutral legal definition governing all manner of sexual assaults must exclude from its definition the gender of sex offenders, their marital status, the specific penetrating object and the specific penetrated orifice.

WHY WOMEN RAPE

Movies, video games, comic books, pornography, rock videos and music lyrics teach consumers that violence equals power. Rape is violent. Therefore, rape equals power. Men and women who rape are expressing their feelings of anger, inadequacy and powerlessness. To feel powerful, a rapist needs to possess, control and dominate. 'Women who commit sexual assaults are largely driven by the same forces as male rapists,' says criminologist Ronald B Flowers, who identifies those forces as 'power, hostility, hatred, sadism, violence, alcohol and/or drugs, mental illness and/or opportunity.' Women can be conventionally feminine, yet equally as cold and calculating as their psychopathic male counterparts. Like men, vengeance, greed, jealousy, and sexual thrills motivate their criminal actions.

Research studies on female sex offenders and their motives are scant. One study called Genesis II was conducted in Minneapolis, Minnesota between 1985 and 1987 with the participation of 16 female sex offenders. Most of the participants acknowledged being sexually aroused by their victims or by fantasies of their victims but claimed that sexual arousal was not a main motivating factor. Their fantasies involved having power in relationships. 'Having sex with my sons was more enjoyable than having sex with a man and that was because I had some control over what was happening,' said one of the participants. Four of the women believed their sex acts were expressions of love either for their victims or their husband-accomplice.

Whether we like it or not, socially unacceptable fantasies and forbidden dreams are part of the human experience. Women who rape and kill feel compelled to act out their fantasies and lack the constraints to keep their impulses in check. They come from backgrounds that are often plagued with extreme emotional, physical and sexual abuse. By asserting their supremacy over a helpless victim, they try to compensate for their own deep seated feelings of worthlessness, inadequacy and inferiority.

THE EXCUSES

'Love' is the most common excuse women use to explain their sex crimes. Unlike male sex offenders, the vast majority of female sex offenders believe they acted out of love for their victims or love for their partners-in-crime. Sex killer Charlene Williams, who participated in the abduction, sexual assault and murder of at least 11 people with Gerald Gallego, explained that her 'love' for Gerald and 'needing someone' motivated her crime spree. Mary Letourneau, who served seven-and-a-half years for child rape, told NBC's 'Today Show' that her relationship with her underage lover was a relationship of 'mutual consensual love'. In 1997, Kim Tran, who put a stop to her philandering husband's affair by cutting off his penis with a meat cleaver and flushing it down the toilet, told police, 'I did it because I loved him so much.' Serial sex killer, Karla Homolka, despite her confessions of an obsessive, everlasting love for her husband-accomplice, Paul Bernardo, pinned the blame on him and plea-bargained a reduced sentence. She concluded that her only crime was 'meeting the wrong man'.

Pre-menstrual syndrome (PMS) has been successfully used as an exonerative excuse in criminal cases by tracing women's violent behaviour to mood swings, irritability, bloating and cramping. At Lizzie Borden's murder trial in 1893, her defense lawyer raised the hormonal argument to explain her axe murders. Since the vast majority of PMS-ing women don't kill, rape or throw vases, few criminologists and doctors subscribe to the belief that raging hormones are the villains in lawless female behaviour. The assumption is that violent women are exceptions to the female rule.

Men have historically used the 'loose excuse' for rape by suggesting that women 'asked for it'. They blame their out-of-control sexual violence on a woman's 'promiscuous past', 'loose morals' and 'provocative dress'. In the 1970s, Lenore Walker gave women an 'abuse excuse' with her claim that battered women become so demoralized by the abuse that they are too helpless to help themselves and conclude that their only option to stop the abuse is to kill the abuser. The abuse-excuse suggests that 'he deserved it'. The 'loose-excuse' suggests that 'she asked for it'.

THE FLIP SIDE OF LOVE

We are a society in love with love, yet 'a lot of what goes on in the name of love has more to do with hate, anger and rage than it does with love', says Dr Jane Goldberg, a New York psychoanalyst. In her book, *The Dark Side Of Love*, Goldberg explains that 'when we have been hurt, betrayed, or abandoned, and when we allow ourselves to feel our hate and rage, the idea of revenge is, as they say, sweet.' As children, we learn that it is morally wrong to 'get even' and to take justice into our own hands. 'Although we think we shouldn't want revenge, we do anyway. As a theme in entertainment, revenge is so popular . . . because characters are depicted doing what we all want to do,' says Goldberg.

The so-called 'entertainment industry' is supported by millions of fans and billions of dollars every year. From racing car crashes to boxing ring knockouts to shoot-'em-up movies, violence entertains and excites us, repels and horrifies us all at once. The violence of blockbuster movie heroes wronged by villains triggers our hate feelings and our desire for revenge. The desire for revenge, says Goldberg, can be a constructive healing process for hurt and anger as long as our violent fantasies remain fantasies. It helps us use our thoughts, feelings and imagination to rein in our impulses and control our actions.

Rape is mismanaged hate. When we imagine rapists suffering the same fate as their victims, we are experiencing the same hateful emotions and fantasies that rapists experience. What separates us from rapists and killers is our ability to manage our hatred by not acting on our hate fantasies. Instead of hating, disowning or burying our own hate, we need to recognize it, own it and find non-destructive outlets for it so that we can 'hate successfully', says Goldberg. Hating cruelty, injustice, poverty and inequality is healthy, justifiable hatred.

It motivates us to defend ourselves and take action to correct it.

In the formative years of a child's development, children experience powerful urges and fantasies to injure and destroy people who disappoint, frustrate and hurt them. 'At their worst, children kick, bite, and tease; they tear off the heads of dolls and squash bugs, draw on walls, crash tricycles,' observes Goldberg, who warns that a parent's reaction of 'horror' to a child's destructive behaviour is as damaging as a parent's 'acceptance' of a child's destructive behaviour. Families who disown their own as well as their child's hatred by suppressing it – fail to teach their child how to use hate constructively.

Karla Faye Tucker turned to drugs and prostitution as a child. As an adult, her bad girl label stuck and became a self fulfilling prophecy. Karla was sentenced to death for two pickaxe murders in Texas and gained notoriety as a paradox of evil and saintliness after she found God on death row. Appeals to commute her sentence polarized public opinion into 'thumbs up' and 'thumbs down' camps. Karla Faye Tucker deserved neither horns nor halos from her fans and critics. The hatred that motivated her crimes was justifiable. Her actions were not.

Love and hate. Good and evil. Heaven and hell. Virgin and whore. These dichotomous Judeo-Christian concepts paint an oversimplified, two-dimensional picture of reality. Thinking in black and white absolutes and failing to recognize that every human being can be both hateful and good, bad and loveable at the same time can have disastrous consequences – especially for children who grow up with the negative labels of verbal abuse. Hating hate is hating a dimension of ourselves that is an inescapable part of our genetic and biological make-up. It is not something we can outgrow or deny any more than we can outgrow or deny love, yet most of us are unskilled in the constructive management of our hate feelings.

SUGAR AND SPICE

In her book, *When She Was Bad*, Patricia Pearson slams, kicks, stomps on, pulverizes and chokes the life out of the modern myth that women are non-violent by nature. Criminologists explain away women's violent criminal behaviour as involuntary or 'the rare result of provocation or mental illness, as if half the population of the globe consisted of saintly stoics who never succumbed to fury, frustration or greed.' An outspoken critic of chivalry justice, Pearson asks the question, 'How can a woman be simultaneously helpless and homicidal?' Although female crimes of violence are rising twice as fast as men's violent crimes, women's acts of aggression are still being dismissed as trivial. Women are not expected to be capable of fighting back or of fighting at all. They are taught to apologize for their strengths while men are taught to apologize for their weaknesses.

Richard Doyle, President of the Men's Defense Association, claims that women are the initiators of violence at least as often as men. In fact, he says, 'the figures show that wives murder their husbands more often than husbands murder their wives and it's seldom in self-defense.' Lenore Walker, who conceived of 'The Battered Woman Syndrome', explains that many women who murder their abusive mates come from homes where violence was an accepted part of everyday life. They reach a breaking point because they never learned the coping skills to deal with anger. 'Most of the women I've dealt with,' says Walker, 'have used guns. The man's gun, to be precise.'

The sexual revolution, affirmative action, feminism, abortion rights and birth control have transformed women's traditional status as housewife and uterus into an option instead of a destiny. With 'Xena' fit bodies and take-no-crap attitudes, women are flexing and 'boxercising' their way into the new millennium. They are signing up for martial arts, aerobics and body-building classes, 'padded attacker' and 'cardio combat' courses. They are arming themselves in record numbers, pumping iron and competing in basketball, hockey and professional contact sports. On the battlefield, women have proven beyond a shadow of a doubt that they can maim, wound, torture, kill and toss grenades without mercy and that an appetite for deadly violence is not gender specific. In Islamic and third-world countries, women are planting bombs, killing and blowing themselves up in suicide bombings. Female terrorists in the Palestinian Intifada, the Irish Republican Army and the German and Italian terrorist movements have blown to smithereens every conceivable myth about female helplessness.

'It does us a disservice to deny our capacity for violence because then we inevitably deny our power as well,' says Elizabeth Herron, co-author of *Gender War, Gender Peace*. Freda Adler, professor of criminal justice at Rutgers University, predicts that as women adopt more traditionally masculine methods of self-empowerment, female aggression and criminality will catch up to men. Since 1980, the number of women sentenced to US prisons has surged by nearly 400 percent. 'Women are committing more aggressive crimes, more violent crimes and that trend is expected to continue,' says Adler who dismisses the view that women are non-aggressive by nature. Karla Homolka, Mary Letourneau, Lorena Bobbitt, Pamela Smart and Karla Faye Tucker have not only dismissed that view, they have assaulted, gang banged and pickaxed the daylights out of it.

BIBLIOGRAPHY

Badinter, Elisabeth, *The Unopposite Sex*, New York: Harper & Row, 1998

Briggs, Freda, *From Victim To Offender*, NSW: Allen & Unwin, 1994

Burnside, Scott, *Deadly Innocence*, New York: Warner Books, 1995

Clarkson, Wensley, *Caged Heat*, New York: St. Martin's Press, c 1998

Codrescu, Andrei, *The Blood Countess*, New York: Simon & Schuster, c 1995

Cole, Susan G., *Pornography and the Sex Crisis*, Toronto: Second Story
    Press c 1989

Davey, Frank, *Karla's Web*, Toronto: Viking, 1991

Davis, Elizabeth, *Women, Sex and Desire*, Alameda, CA: Hunter House c 1991

Edwards, Susan, *Female Sexuality and the Law*, Oxford: M. Robertson, 1981

Faludi, Susan, *Backlash*, New York: Crown, c 1991

Farrell, Warren, *The Myth of Male Power*, New York: Simon & Schuster, 1993

Flowers, Ronald B., *Female Crime, Criminals & Cellmates*, Jefferson, NC:
    McFarland & Co., 1995

Goldberg, Jane G., *The Dark Side of Love,* New York: G.P. Putnam's
    Sons, c 1993

Heidensohn, Francis M., *Women and Crime*, Washington Square, New
    York, New York University Press, 1995

Hite, Shere, *The Hite Report*, London: Pandora, 1989

Janus, Samuel S. and Cynthia L. Janus, *The Janus Report*, New York:
    Wiley, c 1993

Jones, Ann, *Women Who Kill*, Boston, Mass., Beacon Press, 1996

BIBLIOGRAPHY

Kaminer, Wendy, *I'm Dysfunctional, You're Dysfunctional*, Reading, Mass: Addison-Wesley, c 1992

Kane, Peter, *The Bobbitt Case: You Decide*, New York: Pinnacle Books, 1994

Kasl, Charlotte Davis, *Women, Sex and Addiction*, New York: Ticknor & Fields, 1989

Kipnis, Aaron and Elizabeth, Herron, *Gender War, Gender Peace*, New York: Morrow, c 1994

Lehrman, Karen, *The Lipstick Proviso,* New York: Anchor Books, c 1997

Lord, M.G., *Forever Barbie,* New York: Morrow & Co., c 1994

Lowry, Beverly, *Crossed Over,* New York: A.A. Knopf, 1992

Martin, Del, *Battered Wives*, San Francisco: Glide Publications, c 1976

Mathews, Ruth and Kathleen, Speltz, *Female Sexual Offenders,* Orwell, VT: Safer Society Press, c 1989

Maynard, Joyce, *To Die For*, New York: Dutton, 1992

Mortimer, John (Editor), *The Oxford Book of Villains,* New York: Oxford University Press, 1992

Myers, Alice and Sarah, Wright, (Editors), *No Angels*, London: Pandora, 1996

Paglia, Camille, *Vamps and Tramps,* New York:Vintage Books, 1994

Pearson, Patricia, *When She was Bad*, Toronto: Random House of Canada, 1997

Pron, Nick, *Lethal Marriage,* New York: Warner Books, 1995

Schechter, Harold and David, Everitt, *The A to Z Encyclopedia of Serial Killers*, New York: Pocket books, 1996

Weisbrot, Robert, *Xena Warrior Princess,* New York: Doubleday, 1998

Wilson, Colin and Donald, Seaman, *The Serial Killers*, London: Virgin Publishing Limited, c 1990

Wylie, Betty Jane, *Men! Quotations About Men By Women*, Toronto: Key Porter Books, 1993